Ready-to-Use
Tools & Materials for Remediating Specific Learning Disabilities

VOLUME II

COMPLETE LEARNING DISABILITIES RESOURCE LIBRARY

JOAN M. HARWELL

Illustrations by Colleen Duffey Shoup

**THE CENTER FOR APPLIED
RESEARCH IN EDUCATION**
West Nyack, New York 10994

Library of Congress Cataloging-in-Publication Data

Harwell, Joan M.
        Complete learning disabilities resource library : ready-to-use
tools & materials for remediating specific learning disabilities, volume II
/ Joan M. Harwell.
            p.   cm.
        Includes bibliograpbical references.
        ISBN 0-87628-280-X
        1. Learning disabled children—Education—United States.
    2. Learning disabled children—Services for—United States.
    3. Learning disabilities—United States.   I. Title.
    LC4705.H367   1995   95-24094
    371.91—dc20   CIP

Printed in the United States of America

10   9   8   7   6   5

ISBN 0-87628-280-X

**THE CENTER FOR APPLIED RESEARCH
IN EDUCATION**
West Nyack, NY 10994

On the World Wide Web at http://www.phdirect.com

ABOUT THE AUTHOR

Joan M. Harwell has over 30 years of experience as a regular classroom teacher and special education teacher for learning disabled students in the schools of San Bernardino, California. She has run several remedial programs for slow learners and spent 14 years as a learning handicapped Resource Specialist. Currently, she supervises student teachers for the University of Redlands. She is the author of *How to Diagnose and Correct Learning Disabilities in the Classroom* (Parker, 1982), *Complete Learning Disabilities Handbook* (Center for Applied Research in Education, 1989), and *Ready-to-Use Learning Disabilities Activities Kit* (Center for Applied Research in Education, 1993). She is listed in Marquis' *Who's Who in American Education.*

Ms. Harwell earned a B.A. degree from San Jose State College and an M.A. from the University of Redlands.

ABOUT THIS RESOURCE LIBRARY

My purpose in writing the *Complete Learning Disabilities Resource Library*, Volumes I and II, is to share with you some of the things I have learned in my thirty years of working with learning disabled (LD) students, both in mainstreamed classes and in special classes, at the elementary and secondary levels.

When I began teaching special education classes for educably mentally retarded students in 1964, the educational field of learning disabilities was brand new. When I heard the term for the first time, I was immediately able to attach it to three students in my junior high class, who were able to pick up skills more quickly than other students in the class. Although we did not use the term "mainstreaming" in those days, I was able to find teachers willing to have these three students in their regular classes for half the day, where they received extra help and encouragement so they could maintain passing grades. It was with great satisfaction that we—the teachers and the parents—saw those three students go on to complete a vocational nurses' program. As I watched their success, it aroused in me a fierce and abiding interest in the field of learning disabilities.

By 1971, I found myself working with learning disabled students in pull-out programs at the elementary level. In those days, we sincerely believed that if we provided LD youngsters with the right curriculum and concerned teaching, students would overcome or compensate for their disabilities. We would "fix" them. Sad to say, experience over the last 25 years has not borne this out. Students with learning disabilities grow into adults with learning disabilities. Once they leave school, these students find niches where they try to blend in with other adults with varying degrees of success. We now realize how important the parent's role is in determining whether these students will be successful.

Unfortunately, economic and social pressures within today's society have created a situation where parents are not exerting the influence they were able to exert in the 1960s. Parents say they simply do not have time to spend with their children. You will note Volume I continuously mentions the importance of involving parents of LD students in being the children's helpers and advocates. When students are originally identified as LD, do not be afraid or timid to tell parents how critical it is that they maintain weekly contacts with teachers, give encouragement to their children, and offer one-to-one help with their children's assignments at home.

Some parents report that they have never met with the Student Study or I.E.P. teams. Even though the law mandates parent involvement, obviously on occasion some schools are not involving them in any other way than having them sign papers. This is a very questionable practice. It is imperative that you enlist parents' (1) input in planning for their youngster's educational program and future, and (2) help with homework and the teaching of social skills.

The *Complete Learning Disabilities Resource Library* will show you how to involve parents in their LD children's education—and much more!

- Volume I, *Ready-to-Use Information & Materials for Assessing Specific Learning Disabilities*, provides you with a helpful background on the field of learning disabilities. It is intended to assist both the regular class teacher dealing with mainstreamed students and the special education teacher. If you are a beginning teacher, Volume I provides a wealth of information to help you as you begin your work in the field. The book is also of interest to school principals and to medical practitioners as a desk reference. While

Volume I mentions some of the research that has occurred in the field, it does not do so in technical terms; the book is written at a level that is understandable to parents.

- Volume II, *Ready-to-Use Tools & Materials for Remediating Specific Learning Disabilities*, provides you with ready-to-use materials and activities you can use with students in the areas of reading, language arts, and mathematics. The majority of learning disabled students (even those leaving our high schools) have achievement scores that fall in the 1.0 to 5.0 range; for this reason, the difficulty of the materials in Volume II are confined to that range. (Keep in mind that the materials included in Volume II are not intended to replace those supplied by your district; rather, they are supplements. Colleagues have found them particularly helpful as homework.)

I look forward to watching the developments in our field, and am confident we will find more effective ways to help LD students. There are still far too many students who slip through school without acquiring those skills necessary to enable them to feel good about themselves. It is my hope that the information you find in the *Complete Learning Disabilities Resource Library* will make a positive difference in what you are able to do to help students.

Joan M. Harwell

ABOUT VOLUME II

Volume II of the *Complete Learning Disabilities Resource Library* is designed to help meet the needs of learning disabled students from kindergarten through high school. These materials are organized by *functional* level rather than *grade* level because LD students function significantly below their grade level. for example:

- at the end of grade 1, functional level is about 1.0-1.4
- at the end of grade 2, functional level is about 1.5-1.9
- at the end of grade 3, functional level is about 1.9-2.3
- at the end of grade 4, functional level is about 2.3-2.8
- at the end of grade 5, functional level is about 2.9-3.4
- at the end of grade 6, functional level is about 3.5-3.9
- at the end of grade 7, functional level is about 4.0-4.5

It is typical for LD students to show less than a half year's growth for each year of schooling. It is also typical for them to do even poorer as time goes on so that by the time they are seniors in high school, their achievement levels are at about the fifth- or sixth-grade level.

Take a moment to look through this book so that you know what tools and materials are included. If you are

...an elementary Resource Specialist (Rsp), you will be able to use everything in this book.

...a junior high or senior high Rsp, you will primarily use Units 3 through 6. Even if the student is functioning at a fifth- or sixth-grade level, you will still find these materials valuable in terms of building skills.

...a special day class teacher, these materials will help you enormously. Your students often show an even greater range of achievement, so it is not uncommon to have students who are functioning from 1.5 to 6.0 in a senior high special day class.

...a regular classroom teacher who has mainstreamed or inclusion students, this book will provide alternative materials for meeting individual needs as well as homework materials for your special students. You may even find some of the materials appropriate for use with *all* your students.

...a parent, the ideas presented here are easy to follow, so you may want to work your child through the materials.

For some skills, such as alphabetizing, two ready-to-use dittoes are provided. Although that number is not sufficient to teach the skill, it will give you a model from which you can devise your own to reflect the needs of your particular students.

In short, the underlying principles of Volume II are:

- Decide what you are going to teach.
- Believe that the student can learn it.
- Work on it every day until it is mastered.
- Get feedback.
- Give lots of encouragement.

You will get results!

ACKNOWLEDGMENTS

I would like to thank the following persons (all were my colleagues in the San Bernardino City Unified School District) for their help in compiling this book:

Dr. Neal Roberts, Superintendent of San Bernardino City Unified School District

Colene Pate, Pat Wright, and Linda Paule, Program Specialists

Sharon Kilpatrick and Sandy Laurenco of the Early Childhood Program

Sheila Berger, regarding technology

Diane Wheeler, Director of Psychological Services

Pat Kimerer, Psychologist

Marge Lumbley, Parent Liaison

Clifford Harwell and Ann Land, middle school teachers

Janet Nickel, high school resource specialist

Bobbie Pregmon, Principal, Thompson School

Suzi Negron, Counselor

Connie Carlson, Tutorial Assistant

Chris Le Roy, Transition Office

Marion Klein, Director of Special Education

CONTENTS

Unit 6   Materials for Teaching Advanced Writing 327

1

MATERIALS FOR CHILDREN AGES 3 TO 7

OBJECTIVES FOR YOUNG STUDENTS

If you must write an I.E.P. for a child, age 3 to 5, the objectives written may parallel the kinds of skills reflected in your observation or those on the dittoes. Here are some of the possibilities that may be considered:

- _____ will be able to cut along wavy and straight lines with a measure of efficiency (the edge is smooth, not jagged; the cut is more on the line than off; the task can be handled in a short time; and the student is not struggling while doing it).

- _____ will color a large object with some degree of proficiency (color is within the lines most of the time; strokes are appropriate—uses small strokes in small spaces, larger strokes for larger spaces, and round strokes for circular items).

- When shown the colors red, blue, green, yellow, black, brown, purple, orange, pink, white, _____ will correctly identify at least eight.

- Given a stack of eight 2-inch blocks, _____ will build a tower at least six blocks high.

- _____ will say six nursery rhymes verbatim from memory (missing no more than one word in each).

- _____ will use a pencil to trace a large object (production shows adequate pressure exerted—does not draw weakly or break point; is on the line most of the time; draws slowly in an effort to be accurate).

- _____ will follow five one-step and five two-step directions with 80% accuracy.

- _____ will be able to look at five common objects (stamp, coin, hand spade, fork and towel) and tell what each one is used for.

- _____ will demonstrate the ability to look at ten items and classify them into three categories (clothes, food, toys).

- _____ is able to sit and listen to a story read for a 5-minute session (standards include: group setting; student looks at teacher or book most of the time; does not touch others; and can tell the teacher what the story is about).

- When an adult is reading to the child, _____ will turn pages in a book when told to do so, demonstrating the understanding that books are read front to back. When asked to "follow" along, child moves finger left to right (at this point we do not expect the child to always be on the right word).

- _____ can accurately count orally from 1 to 10.

- _____ can count sets of blocks from 1 to 10 presented in random order. (Student moves blocks while counting to prevent miscounting.)

- When asked to draw a person, _____ will draw a person, clearly showing at least a head (with two eyes, a mouth) and a body (two legs, two arms). Child will name each body part.

- _____ will understand the concept of taking turns, can wait, raises hand at least 50 percent of the time.

The materials in this section will help you assess what kindergarten children can do. They may be used at the beginning of the year as a diagnostic tool and again at the end of the year to determine whether youngsters are ready to go on to first grade. At the beginning of the year, you will find out whether the child has been exposed to nursery rhymes, using crayons, cutting along lines, and numerous other skills we have determined are prerequisite skills that must be learned before formal academics are begun. At the end of the kindergarten year, after doing all of these types of activities *multiple times* during the year, the child should be able to do all the activities with confidence and without significant difficulty.

If you want materials of a similar nature for *daily practice*, see my book *Ready-to-Use Learning Disabilities Activities Kit* (West Nyack, NY: The Center for Applied Research in Education, 1993).

FORM FOR REPORTING ASSESSMENT RESULTS

On the following pages you will find a guide and a scripted interview you can use during the assessment process. Figure 1-1 will help you obtain and record vital information that you will share with other members of the multi-disciplinary team.

Do the assessment in the child's classroom if possible. Find an area out of the traffic pattern space to use. Be friendly and relaxed. Tell the child you would like to play with him or her for a while to see what he or she can do.

Name _____

FIGURE 1-1

Pretest ☐
Posttest ☐

Child's date of birth _____ Age at time of testing _____

1. Reason for Referral_____

   _____

   _____

2. Right-handed/Left-handed (circle) _____

   _____

   _____

3. Gross Motor Development

   (runs) _____

   (skips) _____

   (hops on one foot) _____

   (catches a 10″ ball from 5 feet away 4/5 times) _____

4. Fine Motor Development

   (uses crayons) _____

   _____

   (uses scissors) _____

   _____

   (builds with blocks) _____

   _____

   (folds paper in half from model) _____

   _____

   (makes figure after watching it modeled)_____

   _____

5. Listening Skills/Memory Skills

   (nursery rhymes) _____

   _____

   _____

Name _____

FIGURE 1-1
(CONTINUED)

(repeats sentences) _____

_____

_____

(follows directions)_____

_____

_____

6. Draw a Person (name and label parts child identifies)

_____

_____

_____

7. Color Identification

_____

_____

_____

8. Naming Common Objects

_____

_____

_____

9. Recognizes Likenesses/Differences

_____

_____

_____

10. Classification

_____

_____

_____

Name _____

FIGURE 1-1
(CONTINUED)

11. Association

_____

_____

12. Counts

(counts from _____ to _____ accurately)

_____

(recognizes written numbers)

_____

(matches number to sets of objects)

_____

13. Pre-literacy Skills

(follows print in a left-to-right sequence/top to bottom of page)_____

_____

(shown a word on a piece of paper, child can find that word when presented on a page

with others) _____

_____

14. Language Development

_____

_____

_____

_____

_____

15. Attention

_____

_____

_____

Name _____

FIGURE 1-1
(CONTINUED)

16. Relationships with Peers

_____

_____

_____

_____

_____

_____

17. Other Concerns

_____

_____

_____

_____

_____

_____

_____

_____

Report prepared by _____

Use the following information to help you gather the data. During the observation, there are two things you want to be sure to do:

- When you place a toy or any material in front of the child, always place it in the center. Record whether the child picks it up with the right hand or left hand. At the end of your session, you will tally the marks you make and record which hand the child uses more often.

- When you ask a question, always try to write the student's answer verbatim. This information will help you evaluate his or her language development for the extent of vocabulary, knowledge of syntax/general information, and articulation errors.

SCRIPTED DIRECTIONS FOR OBSERVING

Here are step-by-step directions and script for using the assessment form given in Figure 1-1.

1. *Reason for Referral:* You will want to interview the referring teacher, if possible. In a one-to-one discussion, teachers often give more detailed information than they are willing to put in writing.
2. *Right-Handed/Left-Handed:* At the end of your session with the child, record the results of your tally (for example, 15:3) and circle which hand was more often used.

For the rest of the interview, follow the script given here:

Begin the interview by saying: **"My name is _____. Are you __(use the child's name)__ ? Let's go over here and play."**

- Put out ten square stacking blocks and ten rectangular blocks, laying them directly in front of the child.

  "Do you like to play with blocks?" Record child's answer verbatim.

  "What do you like to do with blocks?" Child will either answer or show you. Record response.

  "Do you play with blocks at home?" Record response word for word.

- Allow the child to play a few minutes without direction. Record what child does—lines them up? makes towers? makes bridges?

- Take five blocks and stack them. **"Can you do this?"** Once the child does it, say: **"How many blocks did I put out?" "How tall can you make that tower?"** As the child builds his or her tower, ask the child to count the blocks he or she used. Record whether child can count. Continue to tally which hand child uses to pick up each block. When the tower collapses, say, **"You did very good."**

- Put out four small cars. Let the child play with blocks/cars as he or she wishes for a few minutes without direction. Record what child does—mouth noises? crashes them together? builds garages? etc. Ask, **"How many cars do you have?"** After a few minutes, say: **"Let's do something else. Can you put the blocks in this container and the toy cars in here?"** Record whether child could do it.

- Put out a marker and a paper. Ask, **"Can you do this?"** (Draw a vertical line.) Record result. **"Good. Can you do this?"** (Make a horizontal line.) **"Can you do this?"** (Draw a good sized circle.) When the child makes a circle, save the paper to show. Was it the same size as yours? Was it closed? Was it round?

- On a circle, draw two eyes, a mouth, and ears. **Can you name these body parts?**

- Give the child a paper and ask him or her to draw a person. If the child only draws a face, say, **"Can you draw the whole person, not just a face?"** Label each part he or she draws. Save the drawing.

- Ask, **"Can you do this?"** Take a piece of paper and fold it exactly in half as the child watches. Record results.

- Ask the child, **"Do you ever get to cut with scissors?"** Using the reproducible marked Ditto #1, have the student try to cut along each kind of line. Record how the student did. You will want to have both left- and right-handed scissors available.

- Get out a 9-piece puzzle. **"What do you see in this picture?"** Turn pieces out. **"Would you like to try to put it back together?"**

- At this point, the child may be getting restless. If he or she is, take the child outside. Ask, **"How fast can you run?"** Does the child's running look normal? Some children run with a strange gait.

- **"Can you hop on one foot?"** (Demonstrate.) **"Let me count how many times you can hop on that foot."** (Count out loud.) **"Can you hop on your other foot? Let me see. I'll count."** (Count out loud.) **"Can you skip?"** (Demonstrate.)

- You are ready to go inside to finish the observation. Take out Ditto #2. **"Do you know what this is about?"** If the child does not start to say the rhyme, you say, **"Humpty Dumpty sat on a wall… Do you know the rest?"** Record whether the rhyme is said with or without substantive errors.

- Put out four crayons—red, green, blue, yellow. **"What color do you want to color Humpty Dumpty's pants?"** If the child picks up a crayon but doesn't name it, ask, **"What color is that?"**

- Put out the written version of Humpty Dumpty. Take the child's finger and put it on the words. Say, **"Let's read it together."** Direct child's finger over the first two lines, then let go and see if child continues to follow over the next two lines. Record. Give the child credit if he or she moves his or her finger left to right even if he or she isn't on the right word.

- Show the child Ditto #3, which begins with "Old Mother Hubbard. **"Can you say this rhyme?"** Record. There are two others you can ask about if you need to.

- Get out a 10-inch soft rubber ball. Stand about 5 to 7 feet away and say: **"I'm going to throw this to you. Can you catch it?"** Throw it five times. Record how many times the child caught it. If the child doesn't get it four out of five times, record if he or she gets better during a second trial of 5 throws.

- Get out Ditto #4, *Tracing*. Give the child a pencil. **"Can you trace over this broken line? Pretend your pencil is a car and the line is a road. Try to keep your pencil right on the road."** Record results.

- Get out Ditto #5, *Following Directions*. Say, **"This is a boy, book, ladder, tree."** (Point to each item as you say the name.) **"I want you to put a circle around the tree."**

Cover the first line with a piece of paper so the next line is exposed. **"This is a bee, chicken, needle and thread, rug. I want you to put a circle around the needle and thread."**

Cover that line. **"This is a baby, skate, football, and car."** (Point to each item.) **"I want you to put a circle around the skate."**

"Here is a basket, snowman, hammer, and sign. Put a circle around the basket."

- Get out Ditto #6, *Likenesses and Differences*. Show the child the picture on the left. Say, **"Can you find one like it over here?"** (Sweep your finger over the figures on the right.) Mark the one the child points to. If he or she misses it, say, **"Oops. You should have chosen this one."** (It is important here to give the child feedback because young children do not always understand what they are to do on this ditto. If you have been saying "good" all through the session so far, a couple of no's won't unnerve the child.) Record whether the child got the answers right or whether his or her performance improved as he or she got feedback from you.

- Get out Ditto #7, *Classification*. Cover the sheet with clear self-stick vinyl and cut out the pictures. Lay out all twelve pictures so the child can see them. Say, **"Pile the pictures that go together."** If the child doesn't understand, you can put the chicken with the bee. Record if the child is able to categorize the items into groups. If so, ask, **"Can you name this group?"** The groups are animals, food, clothing. Ask, **"Can you name each thing?"** Record the rate that the child uses to name call. If there is hesitancy, record the name of the object the child had trouble with. If his or her whole retrieval rate is slow, say so.

- Get out Ditto #8, *Association*. Say, **"Let's see which of these things go together. The rake is used to rake up the leaves. What goes with the bat?"** Write responses. **"What goes with the brush?" "What goes with the baby?"**

- Get out Ditto #9, *Listening*. **"Can you name all the pictures on here?"** Help if the student needs it. Then proceed to read the words. If the child names only one thing, ask, **"What else can you see at night?"**

The last thing you are going to do is ask the child to repeat what you say. Say each sentence only one time. Record what the child says. If the child cannot repeat it, say, **"Listen carefully because I can only say it once."**

1. **"I am tired."** (child repeats) (3 words)
2. **"Eat your dinner."** (child repeats) (3 words)
3. **"Did you see that?"** (child repeats) (4 words)
4. **"I saw a bird."** (child repeats) (4 words)
5. **"That is a pretty dress."** (child repeats) (5 words)
6. **"Would you like some candy?"** (child repeats) (5 words)
7. **"Can you come over to play?"** (child repeats) (6 words)
8. **"My mom and dad went shopping."** (child repeats) (6 words)
9. **"My teacher is over fifty years old."** (child repeats) (7 words)
10. **"Ask your dad if he wants pie."** (child repeats) (7 words)

Finally, ask the child to write his or her name on Ditto #2 (Humpty Dumpty). If the child cannot, make him or her a model and see if the child can copy that. Record on your form which he or she did.

At the end of the kindergarten year, you will give the same test. You probably will note significant improvement if the child has worked on these skills on a regular basis.

At the end of the year, you will want to see if the child can recognize number symbols and match them with sets showing that number of items. (See Ditto #10 and Ditto #11.) You will also want to see whether the child can:

1. say the alphabet
2. recognize the letters of the alphabet (presented randomly)
3. give the sound of the letters

See Chapter 11, "Teaching Reading," of Volume I.

DITTO #1, CUTTING

Using scissors, cut on the line.

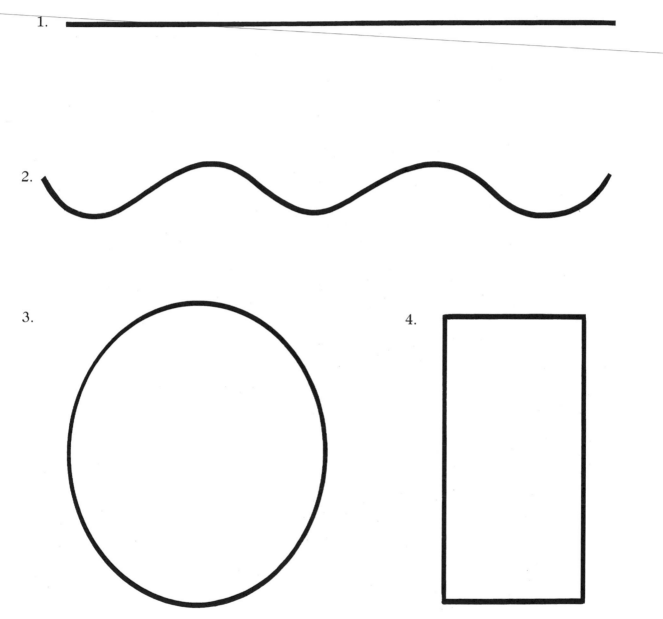

1.

2.

3.

4.

Name _____

DITTO #2, HUMPTY DUMPTY

Humpty Dumpty sat on a wall,

Humpty Dumpty had a great fall.

All the King's horses

And all the King's men

Couldn't put Humpty together again.

DITTO #3, MOTHER GOOSE NURSERY RHYMES

Old Mother Hubbard
Went to the cupboard
To get her poor dog a bone.
When she got there,
The cupboard was bare
So the poor dog got none.

Little Miss Muffet
Sat on a tuffet
Eating her curds and whey;
Along came a spider
And sat down
Beside her
And frightened Miss Muffet away.

Star Light, Star Bright,
First star I see tonight;
I wish I may, I wish I might
Have the wish I wish tonight.

Tracing

Ball

Name _____

DITTO #5, FOLLOWING DIRECTIONS

1.

2.

3.

4.

Name _____

DITTO #6, LIKENESSES AND DIFFERENCES

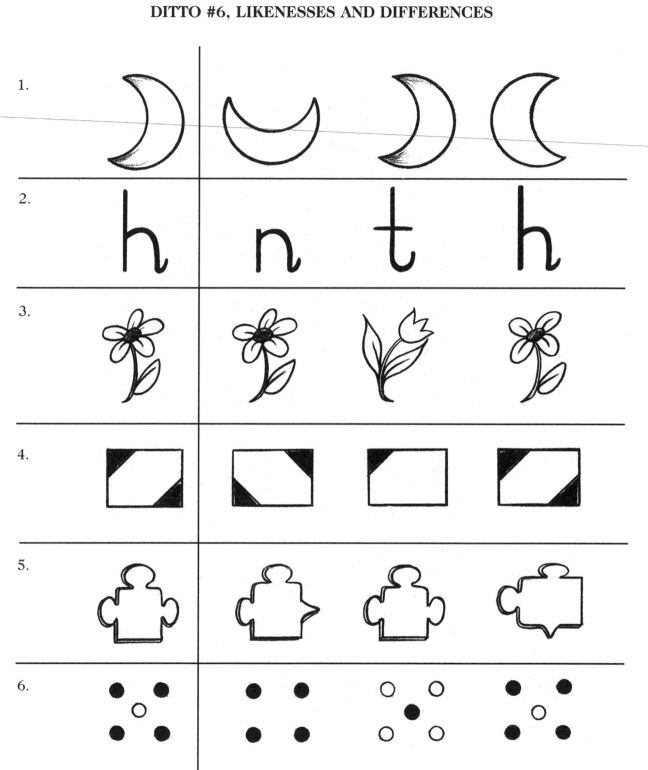

1.

2.

h n t h

3.

4.

5.

6.

DITTO #7, CLASSIFICATION

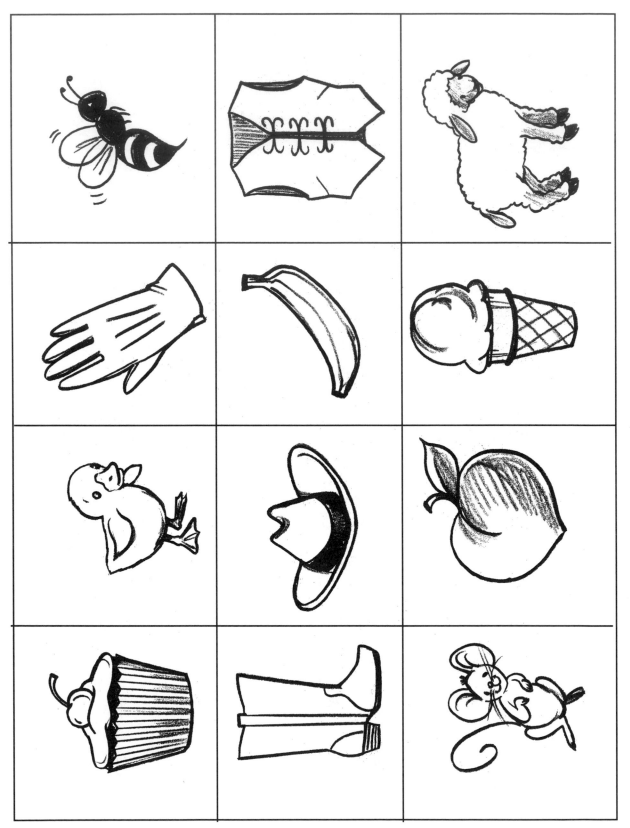

DITTO #9, LISTENING

"Point to two things you could see at night."

"Point to two things you can use to eat your food."

"Point to two things you put on your feet."

"Point to two things you use when it rains."

"Point to two things that can fly."

Name _____

DITTO #10, NUMBERS

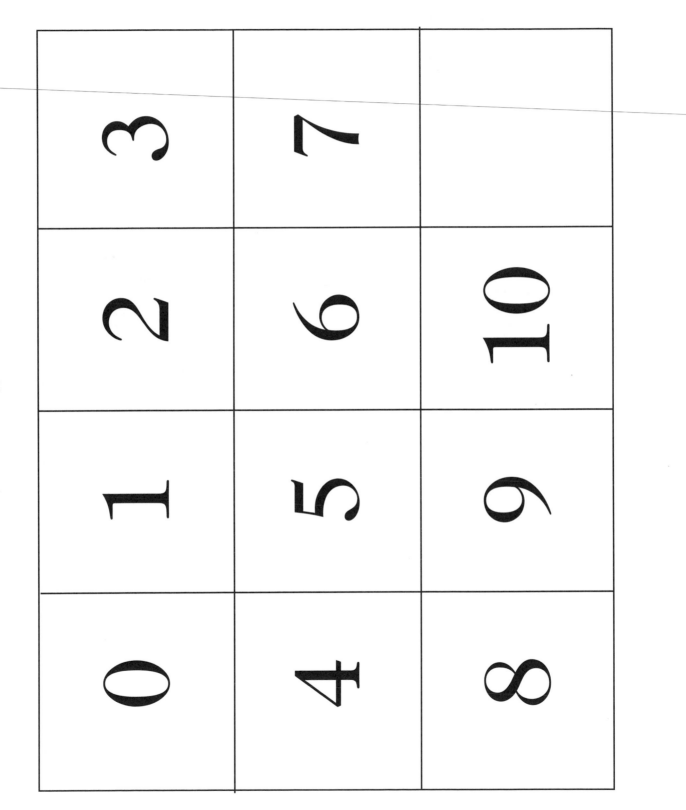

3	7	
2	6	10
1	5	9
0	4	8

DITTO #11, UNDERSTANDING ONE:ONE CORRESPONDENCE

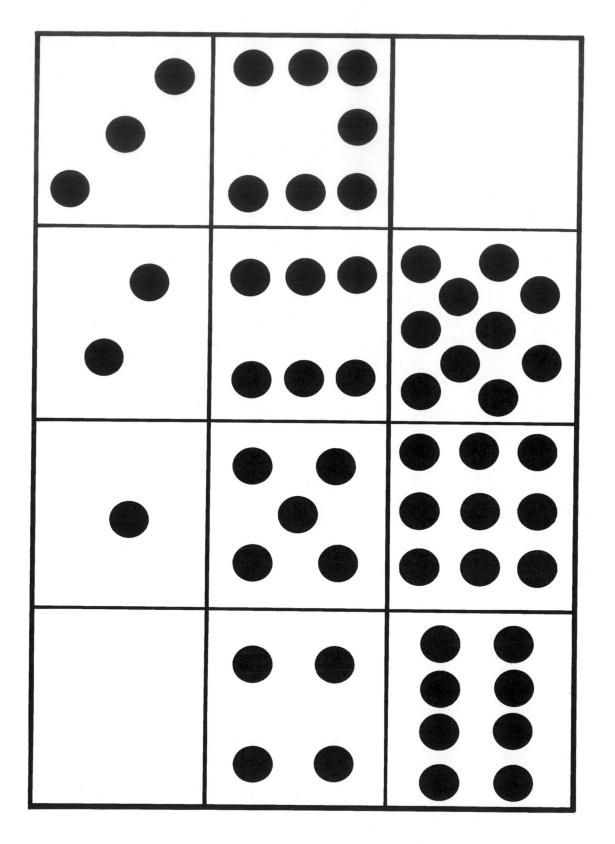

Materials for Teaching Beginning Reading and Language Arts

OBJECTIVES FOR LEVEL 1.0 TO 1.5

Objectives for I.E.P.s for students who are functioning at grade level 1.0–1.5 at the time of assessment are:

- _____ will accurately say the alphabet.

- _____ will be able to name (all / #) alphabet letters (lower case) when presented randomly.

- _____ will orally give the correct sound for (all / #) letters when shown the letter.

- Given a list of 20 words with the vc or cvc configuration, _____ will orally decode the words with 70% accuracy.

- _____ will match color words with the correct color.

- When shown flash cards of first 100 words (presented in random order), _____ will recognize and orally name (#) of words.

- _____ will orally read aloud to an adult 15 minutes per day, receiving immediate feedback and help with unknown words.

- _____ will accurately spell (#) of words from the first 100 words.

- Given six words, _____ will correctly rewrite them in alphabetical order (3 out of 3 trials).

- When 5 sentences are dictated (20 words total), _____ will write the sentences. Each sentence will begin with a capital letter and end with a period. Words will be spelled with at least 75% accuracy.

- _____ will match number words (1 to 10) with numbers.

VOWEL SOUNDS

First, the child must be able to give a sound for each letter of the alphabet. In this section you will find Ditto #12, *Tracing Lower-case Letters/Letter Sounds*, to help you. Say: **"The letter's name is ____. Its sound is ____."** Have the student repeat both the letter's name and its sound.

Using Chapter 11, "Teaching Reading," from Volume I, teach letters and sounds. Cover Ditto #13A and Ditto #13B with clear self-stick vinyl and cut apart the cards. Shuffle the letter cards and let the child put them in correct order. Then shuffle the picture referent cards. Have the child lay the picture-match on top of the letter card.

Next teach the student to draw the referent; for example, the referent for *a* is an apple. Sometimes children will say they can't draw the referents; with encouragement, however, they can—even if their apple is just a circle with a stem. The first day, your progress will be slow since everything you are teaching is new to the children. As you repeat the same activity day after day (same ditto, same format, same information), the child will gain speed. By day 10, you can probably go through the entire ditto in 30 minutes. After you become familiar with the process, you may even find you can do the activity with groups of children. (I have done it with 33 beginning first graders during the first week of school, with three parent assistants who circulate and help the children stay on task or let me know when I need to slow down.)

Each day put up two words and show the children "why" they are learning these sounds. Using simple words such as *in, up, at, cat, dog,* show them how to put the two sounds together to get a word.

By the 20th day, most children have all the sounds; a few stragglers may take up to 40 days. There will come a time around the 20th day when you need to begin to have the child demonstrate he or she can blend sounds together and get words. Some will be able to do it right away, while others will need your one-to-one assistance (modeling) to do it.

In this section, you will find Ditto #14, giving words you can use for this purpose. Cover these cards with clear self-stick vinyl before cutting them out. Along with the group of words that are said exactly as they are spelled, you will find several words that either have a silent letter or are sight words the child needs to learn right away. When the child comes to one of these, have him or her say: **"y–o–u spells you."** (If you wish, you can have a parent volunteer make sets for children to take home so parents can help.)

As children become more familiar with the words, you can construct simple sentences using the words; children are so excited when they begin to read whole sentences. Here are a few of the sentences you can construct with the cards.

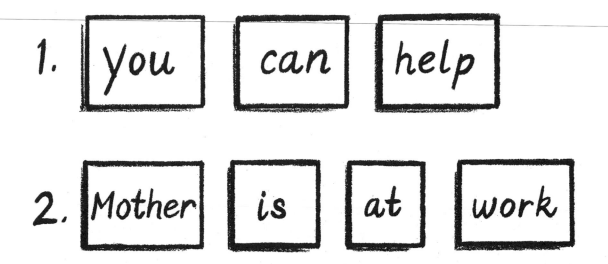

1. you   can   help

2. Mother   is   at   work

Name _____

DITTO #12, TRACING LOWER-CASE LETTERS/LETTER SOUNDS

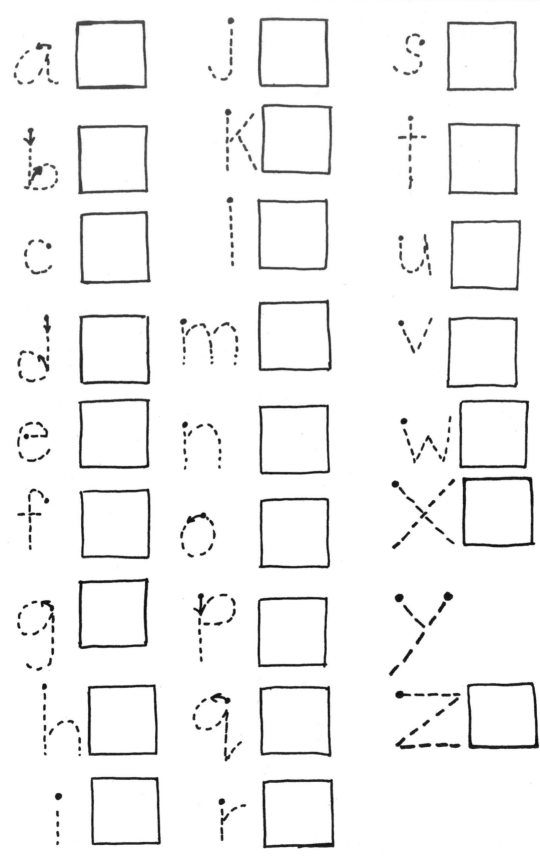

DITTO #13A, ALPHABET LETTERS

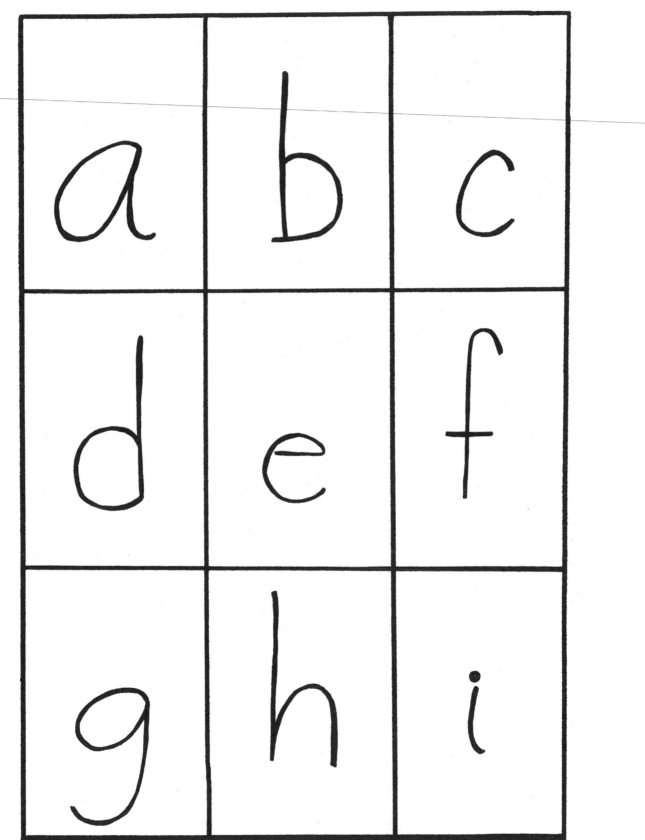

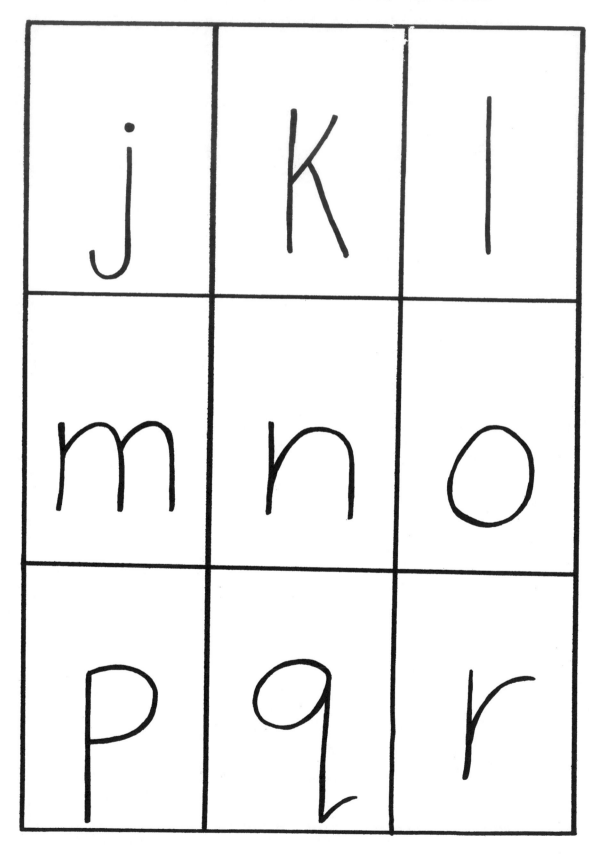

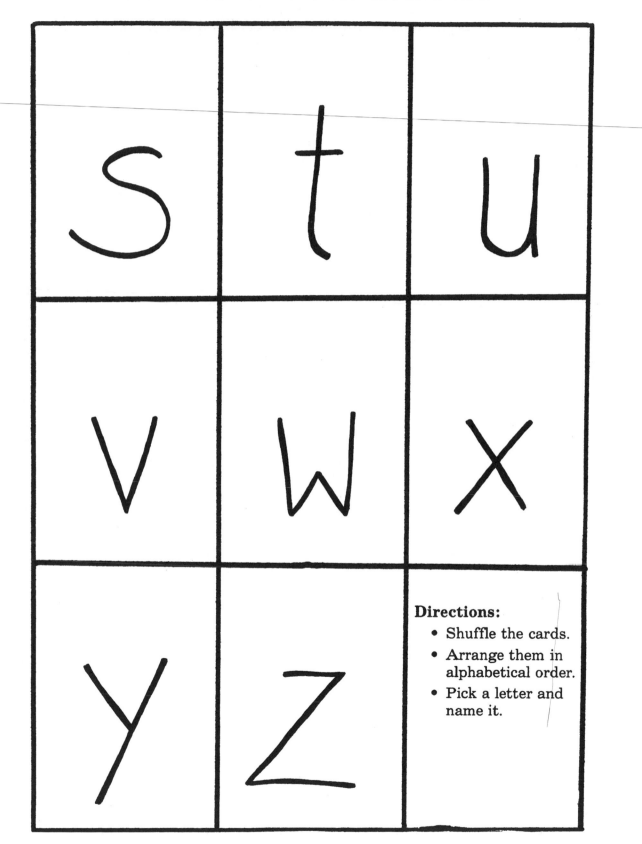

s t u

v w x

y z

Directions:
- Shuffle the cards.
- Arrange them in alphabetical order.
- Pick a letter and name it.

DITTO #13B, LETTER SOUNDS

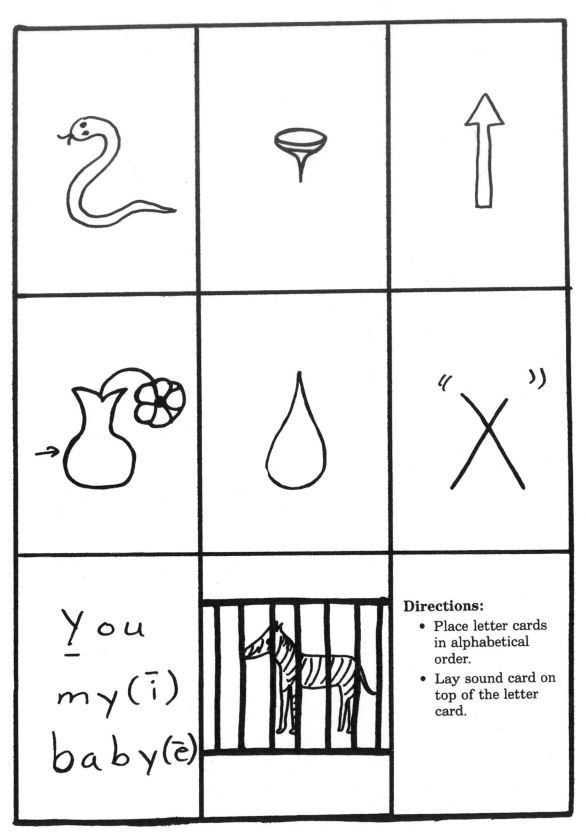

Directions:
- Place letter cards in alphabetical order.
- Lay sound card on top of the letter card.

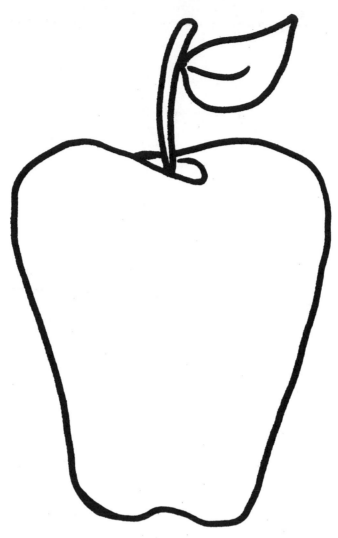

a   apple

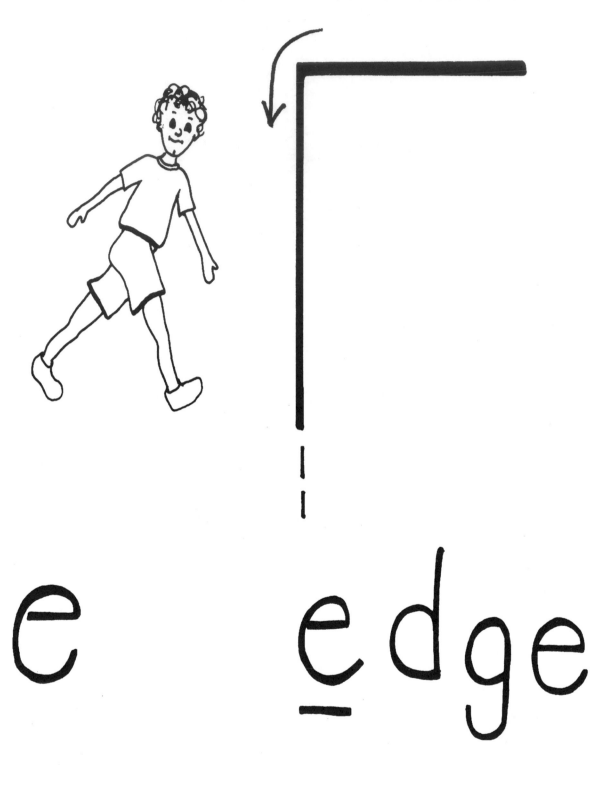

e   edge

i   <u>i</u>tch

o   o̲ctopus

u   <u>u</u>p

BLENDING AND UNBLENDING ACTIVITIES

Teaching fails when the teacher does not spend sufficient time to teach *each* child how to blend the sounds together to get words when the child is reading and how to unblend them when trying to learn to spell them.

Everyday you want to put some completely phonetic words on the board and call on different children to "blend" them. If the child misses, model how it is done. (You will find a list of completely phonetic words in Chapter 11 of Volume I.)

You also need to set aside some time everyday to listen to each child read. Impossible? It may not be possible for *you* to do it, but you *can* train an aide or parent volunteer to do it.

To teach unblending, have children listen to a word you say and then write it on their chalkboard or paper. Before you say the word, tell the children how many letters they are listening for; they can then draw that many spaces on their paper. For example, tell them: **"I'm going to say a word that has three letters. Make three spaces on your paper. (Circulate to see that they do.) When I say the word I want you to listen for the first letter you can hear. The word is dog.** (Really exaggerate the sound of the *d*.) Circulate to see what they wrote. Say: **"Good! Most of you could hear the *d* as in door. If you missed it, change it. Now I'm going to say the word again. This time, I want you to listen for the last letter. Dog.** (Really emphasize the *g* sound.) Circulate as before. Say: **"The sound at the end of dog was a *g*. If you missed it, change it."**

Write the vowels on the board. Review the short vowel sound with the children and draw the referent under each vowel.

"Now we're going to try to listen for the vowel sound in dog. (Stand by the board and point to it.) See which one of these sounds you think you can hear in the middle of dog. (Say "dog," putting the stress on the vowel sound.)

Write *dog* on the board. Have everyone repeat: **"D–o–g spells dog."**

Use the same procedure with each word. Do six to eight words each day. Feel free to reuse ones you have taught before. Remember, the average child needs about 20 repetitions to learn a word.

Teaching Consonant Clusters (sh, th and ch)

We always teach these consonant blends in first grade.

As the children demonstrate they are mastering most of the things you have previously been working on, you can introduce the *sh* sound. When dictating your daily list for unblending, throw in an *sh* word or two. When *sh* is mastered, introduce *th*. The *ch* is the last of the blends you will give. Be sure to include words that have the sound in the initial position—such as *shut*—and in the final position—such as *wish*. If you have trouble thinking of words to use, see the "Resource Word Lists of Special Combinations" in Unit 3 of this book.

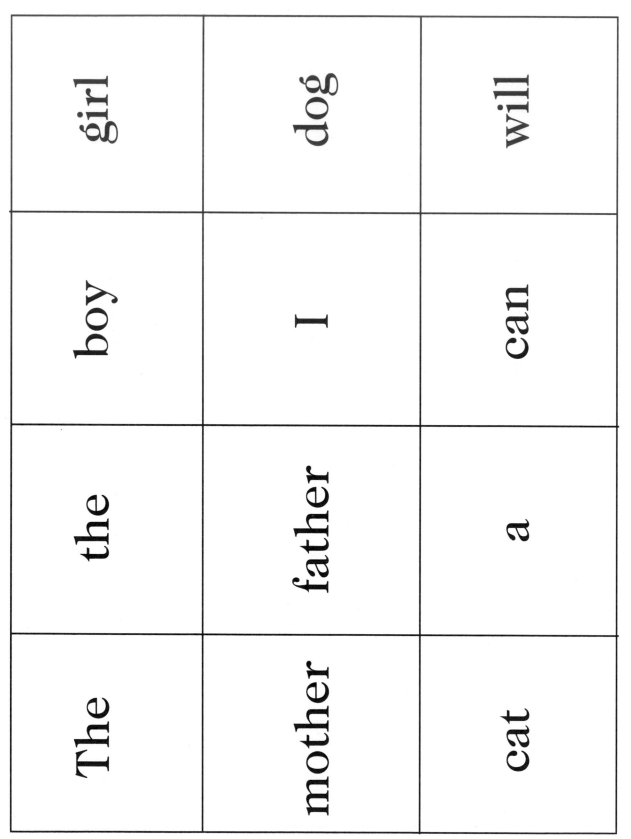

girl	dog	will
boy	I	can
the	father	a
The	mother	cat

help	going	read	to
ball	fast	run	play
not	school	me	gave

want	this	like	do
see	pet	did	what
went	and	home	come

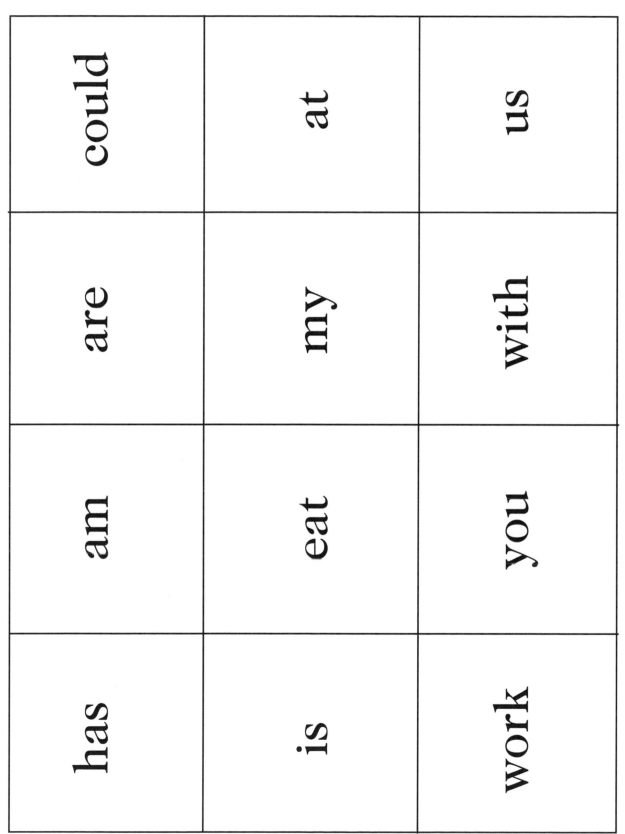

could	are	am	has
at	my	eat	is
us	with	you	work

The "First 100 Most Used Words" Lists

This section offers you the first 100 most used words (functional level 1.0–1.5) along with dictation lessons that require the child to write the words daily. You can begin to teach these sight words by writing them on butcher paper and going over them daily. You say the word and the class repeats it. You will want to discuss how to unblend the sounds. Do a few words each day. After a week of talking about the first 25 words (list), begin the dictation lessons.

When you read the first sentence to them, have the students repeat the sentence at least three times before they try to write it. During the four weeks of dictation, it is okay to have the butcher paper list displayed. At the beginning of week 2, post a list of the second 25 words also and begin to have the students repeat those daily. By the end of four weeks, you will have all 100 words tacked up on the walls of the room. If a child asks you to spell one of those words, send him or her to the list to see if he or she can find it for him- or herself.

Now look at the student worksheet, "Dictation Lesson #1." The sentences for Lesson #1 are:

1. The boy likes to play.
2. The girl likes to play.
3. Mother wants help.
4. The man wants to help.

After you dictate a sentence, have the students repeat it three times and then give them time to write it. You want to give students immediate feedback on how they did. The best way to do this is to go to the board and say: **"I'm going to pretend I am a kid in this class. This is what I would be doing in my head. The sentence is *The boy likes to play.* Hmmm. I know how to spell *the.* Now I know boy starts with a *b* and ends with a *y.* What's in the middle? Well, I can help myself by looking up at the list** (go to the list and point to *boy*). **Oh now I see, boy is spelled b–o–y. Okay, I've got that. *The boy likes to play.* I can find *likes* on the list. I can hear it starts with an *l.* There it is, l–i–k–e. Whoops! What goes in this space? Let me see if I can figure it out. *The boy likes*—oh, I can hear an *s* on the end."**

Write the sentence you dictated on the board. Tell the students to change anything they missed. Circulate to be sure students do.

Now dictate the second sentence. While students are writing, circulate and remind students to look at the posted list if they need to. After a minute or so, put the sentence on the board and tell them to correct their own.

In grading these papers, you can put "Corrected to 100%." The students will learn by making corrections. The student you must worry about and watch is the one who does not make corrections.

As you make each day's dictation form, be sure to make the exact number of spaces the student will need for each word. This provides a critical clue for beginning students.

Sentences for "Dictation Lesson #2" are:

1. Mother wants the boy and girl to help.
2. The girl likes to read.

FIRST 100 MOST USED WORDS

List 1	*List 2*	*List 3*	*List 4*
1. and	1. are	1. all	1. away
2. boy	2. at	2. am	2. blue
3. can	3. but	3. ask	3. every
4. come	4. could	4. do	4. father
5. did	5. doing	5. down	5. from
6. girl	6. eat	6. for	6. green
7. go	7. get	7. good	7. had
8. help	8. going	8. has	8. house
9. like	9. he	9. have	9. how
10. man	10. here	10. him	10. in
11. mother	11. it	11. is	11. just
12. not	12. look	12. keep	12. little
13. out	13. make	13. let	13. much
14. play	14. new	14. me	14. need
15. read	15. now	15. must	15. old
16. see	16. one	16. my	16. put
17. to	17. said	17. of	17. ran
18. the	18. she	18. over	18. red
19. this	19. they	19. so	19. ride
20. us	20. two	20. some	20. run
21. want	21. use	21. that	21. there
22. will	22. we	22. them	22. walk
23. with	23. were	23. thing	23. was
24. work	24. would	24. what	24. went
25. you	25. your	25. why	25. yellow

Name _____

DICTATION LESSON #1

1. ___ ___ ___   ___ ___ ___   ___ ___ ___ ___ ___

   ___ ___   ___ ___ ___ ___ .

2. ___ ___ ___   ___ ___ ___ ___

   ___ ___ ___ ___ ___   ___ ___ ___ ___ .

3. ___ ___ ___ ___ ___ ___   ___ ___ ___ ___ ___

   ___ ___ ___ ___ .

4. ___ ___ ___   ___ ___ ___   ___ ___ ___ ___ ___

   ___ ___   ___ ___ ___ ___ .

3. The boy can not play.
4. The boy will come see the girl.

Sentences for "Dictation Lesson #3" are:

1. The boy and girl like to play.
2. Mother will read to the boy and girl.
3. The man can not help mother.
4. I want you to come play.

Sentences for "Dictation Lesson #4" are:

1. The boy and girl want to go out to play.
2. The man likes to read.
3. Mother can not go. Will you go?
4. I can help you.

Sentences for "Dictation Lesson #5" are:

1. The boy wants to play with the girl.
2. I like to help mother.
3. Mother likes to read.
4. You can come play with us.

Sentences for "Dictation Lesson #6" are:

1. Can you come play with us?
2. The girl will read to us.
3. I want you to come out to play.
4. Mother will not help us.

At this point, post the second butcher paper list of 25 words (List 2) and begin to go over them daily. Single out the following words for particular study—this, one, two, could, would, here.

Sentences for "Dictation Lesson #7" are:

1. Did you see this?
2. One girl and two boys are playing.
3. She could not eat with us.
4. This man wants to see mother but she is not here.

Sentences for "Dictation Lesson #8" are:

1. Come look at this.

2. Did you get the boy to help you?

3. He will read to you.

4. They are going to work.

Sentences for "Dictation Lesson #9" are:

1. Could you help us make this?

2. They said they would come eat with us.

3. I can not read this to you but mother will.

4. "Come here, now!" she said.

On the next day, introduce the concept of word families. Show students how, by changing the first letter in *make*, for example, we can create other words in that family such as *cake, lake, take, bake*.

Sentences for "Dictation Lesson #10" are:

1. Mother said we can make a cake.

2. Would you like to help?

3. She said we were going to see a play.

4. The girl did not look like you.

The next day you will again talk about word families. Show how *look* can be changed to make *book, took, cook*.

Sentences for "Dictation Lesson #11" are:

1. I want to look for a book to read.

2. Two girls are going to the lake with us.

3. He will not come out.

4. She took the book to work.

The next day you will extend the concept of word families. Talk about how you can change *get* to make *pet, let, bet*. You also want to explain that sometimes we add endings to verbs—common endings are *s, ed*, and *ing*. For example, using *look*, show how you can go to look*s*, look*ed*, and look*ing*.

Sentences for "Dictation Lesson #12" are:

1. Could I use one of your books?

2. Would you like to use the new one?

3. They were here but they are not here now.

4. I am going to work now.

On the 13th day, put up List 3 showing the third set of 25 words. Spend some time talking about the word family for *all—ball, fall, hall, tall, wall*.

Sentences for "Dictation Lesson #13" are:

1. Will you do something for me?
2. What would you like for me to do?
3. Could you read this to me?
4. She is a good reader and a good worker.

(Explain the addition of *er*.)

Sentences for "Dictation Lesson #15" are:

1. Let's ask him to come over to eat.
2. I will cook something good.
3. I will need some help.
4. What would you like to have to eat?

Display List 4 showing the final set of 25 words. Remember to review the list daily. Sentences for "Dictation Lesson #16" are:

1. The boy ran away from the dog.
2. I like that old blue house. Do you?
3. Why did she do that?
4. The little girl can not walk.

Sentences for "Dictation Lesson #17" are:

1. Mother said I could come over to play.
2. I can't play. I have to do some house work.
3. How much work do you have to do?
4. I could help you.

Sentences for "Dictation Lesson #18" are:

1. The two boys were going for a walk.
2. The old man did not want to eat.
3. My mother went over to your house.
4. All the boys and girls did good work.

Sentences for "Dictation Lesson #19" are:

1. Did you like that book?
2. I want to read it.
3. The man said he had a good walk.
4. My father likes to run.

By this time you might begin to have individual students name each word on List 1 for a small reward. Have the others clap for them when they can do it.

At this point, you will have used six weeks for teaching sounds, six weeks for blending/unblending practice, and four weeks for familiarizing students with the first 100 words. Now you can begin giving formal spelling lists if you wish. Begin with ten words from List 1; the next week make it 15 words using the original ten plus five more; add five words a week until the children are taking all 25. If you do it this way and don't rush them, they will get a sound foundation while having maximum opportunity to be successful.

THE "SECOND 100 MOST USED WORDS" LISTS

The previous section presented you with a list of the first 100 most used words. Now is a good time to start a notebook for each child so the children can accumulate important papers as their school career goes on. A three-ring binder, which allows the student to add materials, works best because it is very durable. Most parents are willing to buy one; if you scrounge around, you can often come up with ones for students whose parents do not follow through. For young children, the teacher/aide or a parent volunteer must stuff the binder (those rings snap and can be dangerous). Put a copy of the "First 100 Most Used Words" lists and the "Second 100 Most Used Words" lists in the binder and teach children to consult them regularly.

You can make bingo-type games to encourage students to learn to recognize the words. Ditto #15 is a form you can use to make game cards using the 200 words (each card should be slightly different by varying the words or their placement on the cards); the child wins by completing a line diagonally, vertically, or horizontally. A small group of children can play with an aide or volunteer while you are giving instruction to another group. Cut up construction paper squares for the children to cover the words as they are called. The adult supervising the game must keep some record of which words he or she chose to call out for each game. (Those who play might get a cookie; the winner might get two cookies.) If you cover gameboards with clear self-stick vinyl and back them with cardboard, they will last for years. By the time a child has learned to quickly recognize the first 200 words, they are usually reading at beginning second grade.

SECOND 100 MOST USED WORDS

List 1	*List 2*	*List 3*	*List 4*
1. big	1. after	1. about	1. again
2. black	2. be	2. around	2. because
3. came	3. been	3. baby	3. began
4. day	4. does	4. before	4. brother
5. find	5. done	5. best	5. car
6. five	6. friend	6. don't	6. children
7. found	7. garden	7. eight	7. close
8. four	8. give	8. live	8. first
9. gave	9. long	9. more	9. hard
10. grow	10. may	10. never	10. if
11. her	11. morning	11. night	11. kind
12. his	12. next	12. nine	12. left
13. home	13. no	13. once	13. love
14. know	14. on	14. our	14. made
15. many	15. saw	15. school	15. most
16. other	16. seven	16. should	16. name
17. sleep	17. six	17. show	17. open
18. three	18. soon	18. store	18. or
19. under	19. stop	19. talk	19. people
20. up	20. think	20. tell	20. pick
21. very	21. too	21. ten	21. sister
22. when	22. try	22. these	22. then
23. where	23. water	23. those	23. thought
24. white	24. which	24. woman	24. together
25. who	25. yes	25. write	25. upon

DITTO #15, BINGO GAMEBOARD FOR TEACHING WORD RECOGNITION

Teaching Long Vowel Sounds

When a child is *certain* of the short vowel sounds and can accurately and independently blend three to four sounds together and get a word, then it is time to teach the child the long vowel sounds. You will want to display a reminder (Ditto #16) of the common patterns that make a vowel carry the long sound.

Many teachers tell children, "When two vowels go walking, the first one does the talking." Kids parrot it back, but they do not understand what it means or how to use it. Instead, explain to them that the first vowel in the word will say its name if it fits one of these patterns. Use the following list to model how the vowel sound changes in these words:

can—cane	rid—ride	tub—tube	us—use
cap—cape	hope—hope	cut—cute	pin—pine
ran—rain	men—mean	hat—hate	set—seat
rob—robe	dim—dime	kit—kite	fed—feed
bed—bead	cot—coat	slid—slide	got—goat
met—meat	red—read	rip—ripe	net—neat

You can give students a word such as *grow* and have them:

1. Tell you the word.
2. Show you which pattern causes the *o* to say "oh."

If the child encounters a vowel–consonant–consonant–vowel (vccv) word—such as *after*—it will be puzzling unless you explain that when this configuration occurs, it causes the word to break into two syllables: *af* + *ter* (vc/cv).

Learning to Alphabetize by the First Letter of a Word

Using dittoes similar to those of #17 and #18, give students daily practice in alphabetizing words.

When you make your own dittoes, try to use words from the 100 most used word lists.

Allow as many students as you can to name the words to some adult for additional decoding practice.

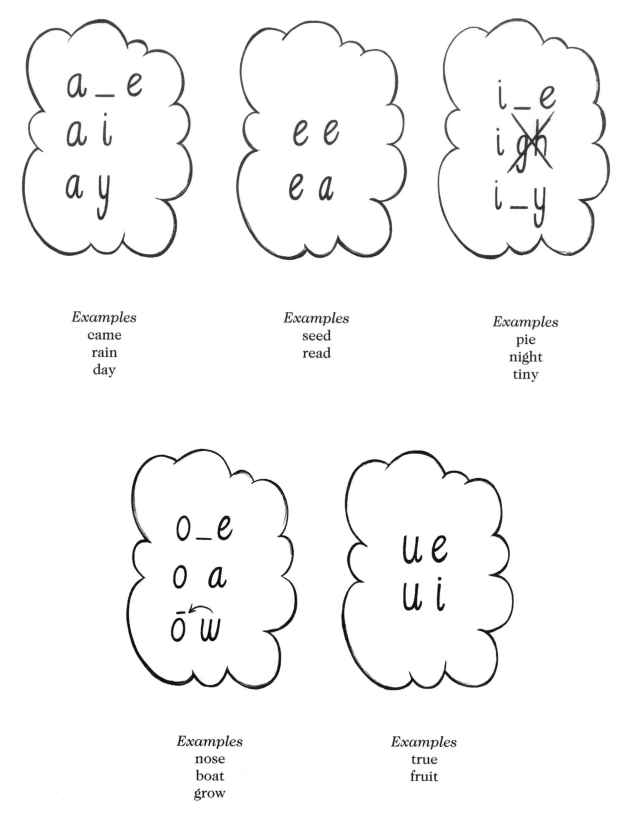

Examples
came
rain
day

Examples
seed
read

Examples
pie
night
tiny

Examples
nose
boat
grow

Examples
true
fruit

Name _____

DITTO #17, ALPHABETIZING

a b c d e f g h i j k l m n o p q r s t u v w x y z

Directions: • Circle the first letter of each word • Alphabetize • Name the words

but	1. _____
has	2. _____
is	3. _____
do	4. _____
let	5. _____
for	6. _____

eat	1. _____
just	2. _____
ask	3. _____
get	4. _____
in	5. _____
can	6. _____

DITTO #18, ALPHABETIZING

a b c d e f g h i j k l m n o p q r s t u v w x y z

Directions: • Circle the first letter of each word • Alphabetize • Name the words

red   1. _____

am   2. _____

said   3. _____

went   4. _____

need   5. _____

here   6. _____

must   1. _____

keep   2. _____

did   3. _____

away   4. _____

put   5. _____

that   6. _____

USING PICTURES TO WRITE SENTENCES

Dittoes #19 through 28 have worked very well for beginning sentence writing. Using old workbook pictures, you can make others. Early dittoes need to carry a word box. Later, after students develop some confidence, they can work from pictures alone.

WRITING SIMPLE STORIES

Writing a story is a very difficult task for LD children of all ages. Initially, you must teach children that all stories have three sections: a beginning, a middle, and an end. Even the most complex novel simplistically has these parts: first, the author introduces us to a situation, then the situation blooms with multiple details, and finally the story comes to an end.

When you begin to teach story writing, students will need a lot of guidance. Using Dittoes #29 through 33, you can have the students write a sentence to go with each picture, putting them together in sequential fashion. Later, you can have the students tell you their 3-part story and then write it. Having aides or parent volunteers available to help can mean the difference between success or failure.

NUMBER WORDS

Using the number words found on Ditto #34, have students learn to match them with the numbers found in Unit 1 of this book. For ways to teach students to spell the words, see Chapter 12, "Teaching Spelling" in Volume I.

COLOR WORDS

Using Ditto #35, have students match a crayon with each color word.

DITTO #19, USING PICTURES TO MAKE SENTENCES

Directions: Make a sentence for each picture. (See the word box at the bottom of the page.)

the girl	is putting	the ball
a man	is smiling	at me
the boy	is hitting	on her skates
	is reading	the newspaper

Name _____

DITTO #20, USING PICTURES TO MAKE SENTENCES

Directions: Make a sentence for each picture. (See the word box at the bottom of the page.)

Some books	are eating	from her hand
the girl	is swimming	the little dog
a puppy	is feeding	on the chair
a cat		from the bowl
		across the pool

Name _____

DITTO #21, USING PICTURES TO MAKE SENTENCES

Directions: Make a sentence for each picture. (See the word box at the bottom of the page.)

the boy	is giving	a gift to her dad
a girl	is sleeping	on a rug
the cat	is sitting	with a boat
	is playing	under a tree

Name _____

DITTO #22, USING PICTURES TO MAKE SENTENCES

Directions: Make a sentence for each picture. (See the word box at the bottom of the page.)

_____

_____

_____

_____

_____

_____

_____

_____

_____

_____

Some children	are swimming	in the rain
a cat	is washing	the van
the man	are walking	on the pond
five ducks	is walking	on the wall

Name _____

DITTO #23, USING PICTURES TO MAKE SENTENCES

Directions: Make a sentence for each picture. (See the word box at the bottom of the page.)

_____

_____

_____

_____

_____

_____

_____

_____

_____

_____

_____

_____

the cat	is riding	down a hill
a goat	is sleeping	a cake
the boy	is walking	in a tree
the man	is baking	down the road
		his bicycle

Name _____

DITTO #24, USING PICTURES TO WRITE SENTENCES

Directions: Using your Word Lists, write a sentence for each picture.

Name _____

DITTO #25, USING PICTURES TO WRITE SENTENCES

Directions: Using your Word Lists, write a sentence for each picture.

_____

_____

_____

_____

_____

_____

_____

_____

_____

_____

_____

_____

Name _____

DITTO #26, USING PICTURES TO WRITE SENTENCES

Directions: Using your Word Lists, write a sentence for each picture.

_____

_____

_____

_____

_____

_____

_____

_____

_____

Name _____

DITTO #27, USING PICTURES TO WRITE SENTENCES

Directions: Can you write a sentence for each picture? Sound out any words that are not on your word lists.

_____

_____

_____

_____

_____

_____

_____

_____

_____

Name _____

DITTO #28, USING PICTURES TO WRITE SENTENCES

Directions: Can you write a sentence for each picture? Sound out any words that are not on your Word Lists.

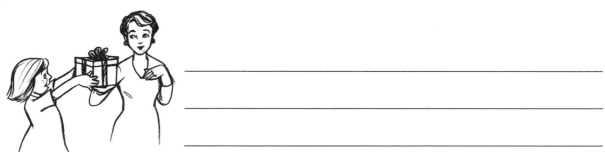

_____

_____

_____

_____

_____

_____

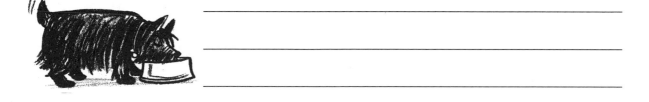

Name _____

A Fish Story

Name _____

DITTO #30, WRITING A STORY—BEGINNING, MIDDLE, END

A New Pet

Name _____

Accidents

Name _____

DITTO #32, WRITING A STORY—BEGINNING, MIDDLE, END

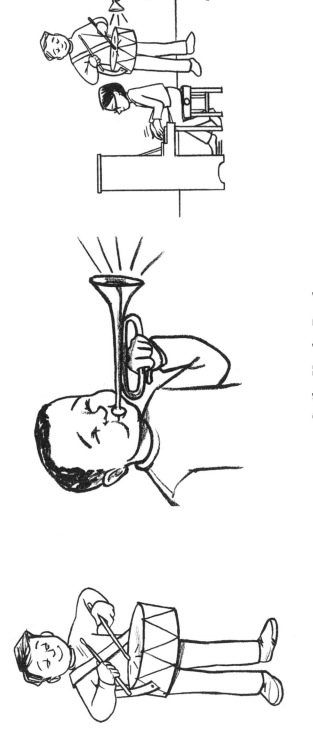

Strike Up the Band

_____

_____

_____

_____

_____

_____

Name _____

DITTO #33, WRITING A STORY—BEGINNING, MIDDLE, END

Draw pictures of the beginning, middle and end.

DITTO #34, RECOGNIZING NUMBER WORDS

three	seven	
two	six	ten
one	five	nine
	four	eight

DITTO #35, RECOGNIZING COLOR WORDS

yellow	purple	
blue	pink	orange
red	black	white
	brown	green

ANTONYMS

Antonyms are words that have opposite meanings. The following list of words makes a good first list to teach.

after—before	fast—slow	in—out
all—none	first—last	
always—never		old—new
ask—tell	give—take	on—off
	good—bad	over—under
back—front		
begin—finish	happy—sad	start—stop
	hard—soft	
come—go	he—she	wet—dry
	here—there	woman—man
dark—light	high—low	work—play
day—night	his—her	
even—odd		yes—no

One of the best activities for teaching antonyms is to take 2″ x 3″ manila cards and write the word on the front and the antonym on the back. You can circulate and give help as students work in pairs, flashing them to each other.

MATERIALS FOR STUDENTS
FUNCTIONING
AT LEVEL 2.0

OBJECTIVES FOR LEVEL 2.0 TO 2.5

Objectives for I.E.P.s for students functioning at level 2.0 to 2.5 at the time of assessment include:

- When shown the lists of the First 100 Words, _____ will orally name 95% of those words correctly.

- When asked to use the "500 Most Used Words" List, _____ will locate 20 words, getting at least 18 right.

- Given three simple story problems, _____ will draw pictures and write an answer, getting at least two problems right.

- When asked, _____ will be able to name at least ten words that signal questions.

- _____ will orally read aloud to an adult (aide or teacher) for 15 minutes each day and receive immediate feedback if a word is missed.

- When asked to look at four simple sentences, _____ will draw a picture for each that shows the meaning of the sentence, getting at least three correct.

- When asked to write the following sentences (dictated—student repeats each sentence three times before writing), _____ will write the sentences with no more than five errors including capitalization, punctuation, and spelling.

  1. We are going out to play.

  2. Mother will go to work.

  3. You are a big girl.

  4. Did you see what I did with my book?

(*Note:* It is assumed the student will not have practiced these specific sentences before, but has had extensive practice with dictation using the first 200 most used words.)

Learning to read reminds me of a train leaving the station. It moves slowly, laboriously at first, but gradually picks up speed. Likewise, readers are very slow in the beginning, when every word has to be figured out. As time goes on, however, readers begin to commit frequently encountered words to memory so they can read faster. The more words committed to memory, the faster their reading speed.

When kids first begin to read, you have to be there to help with every word. When they reach level 2.0 and are familiar with the first 200 words, they may enjoy looking at books. By examining pictures and working out some of the words for themselves, they may be able to get the gist of the story.

As students pick up blending and unblending skills (also called decoding), they need to be encouraged to become "risk takers"—to try to work words out while waiting for the teachers to find time to help them.

RESOURCE WORD LISTS

On the following pages you will find Resource Word Lists that will assist you in providing practice in decoding. Go over a sound combination each day. Put words on the board and have students work them out and explain to their classmates what they did to get the word.

After discussing and working with each sound combination—sh, th, oo, ow/ou, ar—you will find an activity sheet to reinforce the particular sound. You may want to have students read each sentence chorally, following with their fingers.

You can use the bingo-like gameboard found in the previous unit to teach combination sounds by putting the letters in the spaces. As you utter a sound combination (see "Student's Reminder for Decoding" in Unit 4 for possibilities), students mark the letters that make that sound. When you make the *er, ir, ur* sound (same), students can mark all three answers if they have them. Likewise, *ou* and *ow* make the same sound, so students may mark two answers.

Note: Teaching children to decode will not turn them into readers. To become a good reader, a child must spend at least 30 minutes a day practicing reading—15 minutes at school and 15 minutes at home. Materials used will hopefully be at the child's functional levels. If this is not possible, you may want to use the *Neurological Impress method* described in Chapter 11 of Volume I. If this method is used, the child's attention to each word is important. This can be accomplished by using a marker that can be placed under each word or by duplicating the material and having the child underline each word as it is read.

Answers to Activity Sheets:

Ditto #36	Ditto #37	Ditto #38	Ditto #39
1. all	1. shed	1. that	1. zoo
2. tall	2. shut	2. with	2. food
3. fall	3. trash	3. thin	3. tooth
4. call	4. brush	4. think	4. soon
5. hall	5. fresh	5. then	5. broom
6. salt	6. push	6. this	6. pool
7. walk	7. she	7. them	7. school
8. talk	8. fish	8. cloth	8. noon
9. also	9. shop	9. bath	9. tool
10. almost	10. shelf	10. path	10. smooth

Ditto #40	Ditto #41	Ditto #42	Ditto #43
1. how	1. out	1. car	1. chair
2. cow	2. our	2. dark	2. bench
3. brown	3. found	3. park	3. reach
4. town	4. about	4. party	4. cheese
5. crowd	5. pound	5. arm	5. lunch
6. flower	6. cloud	6. sharp	6. chose
7. towel	7. count	7. farm	7. which
8. growl	8. house	8. large	8. chase
9. down	9. scout	9. start	9. each
10. crown	10. loud	10. smart	10. teach

RESOURCE WORD LISTS OF SPECIAL COMBINATIONS

sh (*easy*)

shut	she	ship	shop	shed
shall	shell	shock	dish	wish
splash	rush	fish	fresh	rash
crush	gush	brush	push	trash
cash	mash	sash	crash	flash
dash	hash	hush	shelf	shift
shot				

sh (*harder—long vowel*)

shape	sheet	shade	shame	shake
shine	sheep	shore	shone	leash

sh (*with two or more combinations*)

sh ar p	sh ir t	sh oo t	sh ou t	sh ow
wa sh	sh or t	sh ow er	sh ut ter	

th (*easy*)

this	that	them	then	thick
thumb	think	thank	thus	than
thin	tenth	path	with	bath
cloth	ninth	moth	fifth	math

th (*harder—long vowel*)

these	those	faith	both	teeth

th (*with two or more combinations*)

th un der	th ir d	s ou th	th ing	w or th
th or n	th ir ty	th r ow	th ir st	th r ew

ch (*easy*)

chin	chip	chop	chest	check
catch	much	such	stretch	chick
lunch	inch	chat		

ch (*harder—long vowel*)

chair	chain	chase	cheek	chose
cheap	cheese	cheer	chill	choke
chunk	bench	which	branch	each
teach	reach	beach	beach	bunch
peach	cheat	chime	lunch	

ch (*with two or more combinations*)

ch ie f	ch an ce	ch ar ge	ch ur ch	p er ch
wa t ch	ch an ge	p or ch	ch al k	ch art
ch an t	ch ap ter	ch oi ce	ch oo se	chub by

wa (*as in "water"*)

was	wash	walk	want	watch

RESOURCE WORD LISTS OF SPECIAL COMBINATIONS
(CONTINUED)

oo (*as in "too"*)

soon	tool	loose	pool	cool
food	goose	stool	school	smooth
boot	roof	hoof	room	spoon
scoop	broom	zoo	troop	booth
tooth	noon	tattoo	balloon	shoot

ing

sing	bring	swing	sting	ring
spring	string	thing	wing	finger

ow (*as in "now"*)

how	cow	plow	brown	down
crowd	town	drown	crown	powder
power	scowl	allow	flower	towel

ow (*with **w** acting as a vowel to make **o** say "o"*)

show	slow	owe	grow	flow
follow	bowl	low	below	own
borrow	window	yellow	glow	sown

ew (**oo** *sound as in "new"*)

few	flew	blew	chew	crew
threw	stew	grew		

ou (*as in "out"*)

loud	cloud	count	about	round
sound	hound	proud	around	mouse
house	pound	found	scout	doubt
oust	ground	amount	our	south
mouth	ouch			

ar (*as in "are"*)

car	bar	dark	far	farm
card	jar	hard	mark	bark
part	March	star	smart	carve
arch	art	arm	scar	scarf
start	party	park	yard	sharp
army	shark	charm	chart	large

kn (**k** *is silent*)

knee	knit	knot	knife	knew
know	knuckle	knock		

er (*as in "her"*)

later	after	water	offer	enter
sister	ever	mother	other	winter
better	operate			

RESOURCE WORD LISTS OF SPECIAL COMBINATIONS
(CONTINUED)

ir (*as in "girl"*)

bird	stir	firm	first	dirt
shirt	birth	circle	circus	swirl

ur (*as in "turn"*)

burn	purple	turkey	urge	hurt
surf	during	purse	nurse	curve
curl	occur	hurry	further	curb

or (*as in "for"*)

form	north	orbit	born	order
storm	horse	porch	orchard	cord
fork				

aw (*as in "saw"*)

jaw	claw	paw	hawk	raw
draw	thaw	crawl	law	awful
awning	lawn	yawn	flaw	straw

au (*as in "because"*)

haul	August	auto	faucet	fault
daughter	sauce	caught	sausage	author
audience	laundry	dinosaur	launch	

oi (*as in "oil"*)

boil	soil	broil	point	foil
join	coin	moist	joint	void
hoist	spoil	poison	avoid	

oy (*as in "boy"*)

toy	joy	enjoy	royal	oyster
annoy	decoy	employ		

wr (*w is always silent*)

wrong	wrist	wreath	wreck	wrench

Name _____

DITTO #36, SPECIAL COMBINATIONS ACTIVITY SHEET

Directions: Repeat each word after your teacher. Now name all the words by yourself. Use each word in one of the sentences below. Let the context of the sentence guide you.

all	hall	also	talk	
call	tall	always	walk	(ball)
fall	small	almost	salt	al

1. All birds have wings but not _____ birds can fly.

2. Brian is short but his Dad is _____.

3. If you run and you _____, you may get hurt.

4. When I know I am going to be late, I always give my Mom a

    _____ so she will not worry.

5. "Never run in the _____," the teacher warned us.

6. Some people put _____ on their grapefruit, but I like sugar.

7. Can you stand on your hands and _____?

8. My friend and I _____ too much in class.

9. He drank a soda but he _____ drank two glasses of water.

10. "Don't eat now. It is _____ time for dinner."

Name _____

DITTO #37, SPECIAL COMBINATIONS ACTIVITY SHEET

Directions: Repeat each word after your teacher. Now name all the words by yourself. Use each word in one of the sentences below. Let the context of the sentence help you.

shut	fish	brush	she	
shop	dish	push	shock	sh
shelf	fresh	trash	shed	

1. I want you to get a hoe out of the _____ and help me get the weeds out.

2. Mother got mad when I did not _____ the door and the dog got out.

3. My jobs at home are to take the _____ out and feed the cat.

4. I _____ my hair so it will shine.

5. The bread is soft because it is so _____ .

6. The door sign said "_____ to open."

7. Did you hear what _____ said to me?

8. The _____ swam around the big tank.

9. Mother loves to _____ at the mall.

10. Put the books on that _____ .

Name _____

DITTO #38, SPECIAL COMBINATIONS ACTIVITY SHEET

Directions: Repeat each word after your teacher. Now name all the words by yourself. Use each word in one of the sentences below. Let the context of the sentence help you.

that	with	cloth	think	
this	bath	tenth	thin	*th*
then	path	thick	them	

1. Is _____ your mother?

2. We want you to go _____ us to the mall.

3. She is fat but she wishes she were _____.

4. Do you _____ she likes you?

5. First, do your math and _____ do your reading.

6. Do you want _____ one or that one?

7. The teacher told _____ to line up.

8. The _____ for the new dress mother is making is blue.

9. The dog smells bad. Let's give him a _____.

10. There is a _____ that goes from one side of the park to the other side.

Name _____

DITTO #39, SPECIAL COMBINATIONS ACTIVITY SHEET

Directions: Repeat each word after your teacher. Now name the words by yourself. Use each word in one of the sentences below. Let the context of the sentence help you.

soon	zoo	spoon	broom	
food	pool	room	noon	too
tooth	school	tool	smooth	

1. We will go to the _____ on Sunday.

2. Could you give the dog some _____?

3. I have a loose _____ but I don't want to have it pulled.

4. How _____ can you come help me?

5. Use the _____ to sweep your room.

6. The boy jumped into the _____. He got right out because the water was so cool.

7. We have moved to a new house and I will go to a new

_____.

8. When it is 12 o'clock and time to eat, we say that it is

_____.

9. I can't push this nail in. I need a _____.

10. The cloth feels so _____.

© 1995 by The Center for Applied Research in Education

DITTO #40, SPECIAL COMBINATIONS ACTIVITY SHEET

Directions: Repeat each word after your teacher. Now name the words by yourself. Use each word in one of the sentences below. Let the context of the sentence help you.

how	down	crown	power	
cow	town	towel	allow	
brown	flower	crowd	growl	

1. Did you see _____ she put that box together?

2. Milk comes from a _____.

3. The boots do not show dirt. They are _____.

4. The _____ has a new library.

5. There was a big _____ at the movie.

6. I picked the red _____ and gave it to my mother.

7. Get your hands clean before you wipe them on the

   _____.

8. The dog began to _____ at us.

9. He fell _____ and got hurt.

10. The queen did not put her _____ on for many days.

Name _____

DITTO #41, SPECIAL COMBINATIONS ACTIVITY SHEET

Directions: Repeat each word after your teacher. Now name the words by yourself. Use each word in one of the sentences below. Let the context of the sentence help you.

out	mouth	count	about	
our	cloud	found	house	
loud	pound	around	scout	

1. Take that pin _____ of your mouth, now!

2. Your car is red but _____ car is white.

3. I lost my coat but later I _____ it.

4. It is _____ time to go to bed.

5. You will need a _____ of meat to make that dish.

6. That _____ is black. I think it will rain soon.

7. I need to know how many books are in that box. Can you

   _____ them for me?

8. We live in a big _____ across from the school.

9. Next year, I will be old enough to become a _____.

10. You are being too _____. Dad is trying to sleep.

Name _____

DITTO #42, SPECIAL COMBINATIONS ACTIVITY SHEET

Directions: Repeat each word after your teacher. Now name each word by yourself. Use each word in one of the sentences below. Let the context of the sentence help you.

car	dark	park	sharp	*are*
start	hard	smart	large	
party	arm	farm	yard	

1. My brother is learning how to drive a _____.

2. I must be home before it gets _____.

3. My mother takes me to the _____ on Saturday.

4. We had a good time at her birthday _____.

5. The bee stung my _____.

6. I cut my finger on something that is _____.

7. On the _____, we saw cows, horses, and sheep.

8. Small dogs may bite, but a _____ dog can really hurt you.

9. When he gets mad, he will _____ to cry.

10. You know a lot about snakes. You are so _____.

Name _____

DITTO #43, SPECIAL COMBINATIONS ACTIVITY SHEET

Directions: Repeat each word after your teacher. Now name each word by yourself. Use each word in one of the sentences below. Let the context of the sentences help you.

chair	bench	cheese	chose	*"ch"*
reach	each	chase	branch	(sneezing sound)
teach	lunch	bunch	which	

1. He was leaning back in his _____. It turned over and he fell.

2. While her children play at the park, the mother sits on a

   _____ reading.

3. The toys are on the top shelf, but I cannot _____ them.

4. Most people like to eat _____ and crackers.

5. It is almost noon. I am ready for my _____.

6. There was a red bike and a blue one. He _____ the red one.

7. We have pie and cake. _____ would you like?

8. Dogs like to _____ cats up trees.

9. Please give _____ child a book.

10. After lunch, she will _____ us how to make a kite.

THE "500 MOST USED WORDS" LIST

This is a very important list. Embedded within it are the words that have already been introduced in the First 100 and the Second 100 word lists. If students can learn to recognize and spell these words by the end of grade 6, they will have a good basis for writing. Analysis of adults' everyday writing suggests that these words comprise 75% of adult writing and 90% of student writing at the end of grade 6.

When you hand out the list, you want to give only one page a day. After giving students a sheet of paper, numbered 1 to 20, call out a word. Ask the students to find it and write it on the paper. After they have time to do that, put the word on the board so they can correct their papers. Have a student explain how he or she worked out the word. Call on different students to do each word.

On each day thereafter, give another page of the list and do a similar 1 to 20 activity.

When you have gone over each sheet, spend one day having students locate ten words taken from various pages. You will need to point out that the list is done alphabetically.

The next day, call out ten more words taken from all over the list, collect the papers, and grade them. For students scoring below 8, you will need to create a small group and reteach.

Encourage students to check their list when doing writing assignments. When correcting their own papers, have students circle misspelled words and correct their mistakes.

A

able
about
above
across
afraid
after
again
against
air
all
almost
also
always
am
and
angry
animal
another
answer
any
are
around
as
ask
at
ate

away

B

baby
back
bad
ball
be
beautiful
because
bed
been
before
began
begin
being
believe
below
best
better
between
big
bird
black
blue
book
both
box

boy
bread
bring
brother
brought
brown
build
built
busy
but
buy
by

C

call
came
can
car
carry
cat
catch
caught
cent
change
chase
child
children
city

clean
climb
close
clothes
cold
color
come
cook
corner
could
country
cow
cried
cry
cut

D
daddy
dance
dark
day
deep
did
didn't
different
dig
dinner
dirty
do
does

dog
doing
done
don't
door
down
draw
dress
drink
drive
drop
during

E
each
early
easy
eat
eight
enough
even
ever
every
eye

F
face
fall
family
far

farm
fast
father
feed
feel
feet
felt
few
finally
find
finish
fire
first
fish
five
flew
fly
follow
food
for
found
four
friend
from
Friday
front
fruit
full
fun

funny

G

game
garden
gave
get
girl
give
glad
go
goes
going
good
got
grass
great
green
grew
ground
grow
guess

H

had
hand
happen
happy
has
hat

have
he
head
hear
heard
help
her
here
herself
hide
high
hill
him
himself
his
hold
home
hope
hot
hour
house
how
huge
hundred
hungry
hunt
hurry
hurt

I

ice
idea
if
important
in
is
it

J

join
jump
just

K

keep
kept
kick
kind
kitchen
kitten
knew
know

L

land
large
last
late
laugh

learn
leave
left
let
letter
life
light
like
listen
little
live
long
look
lose
loud
love
lunch

M
made
make
man
many
may
me
mean
men
met
might
mile

milk
mine
Monday
money
more
morning
most
mother
mountain
Mr.
Mrs.
music
must
my

N
name
near
neck
need
neighbor
never
new
next
nice
night
nine
no
noise
north

not
nothing
now
number

O
ocean
of
off
office
often
old
on
once
one
only
open
or
orange
other
our
out
over
own

P
page
paint
paper
park

part
party
pass
penny
people
pick
picnic
picture
piece
place
plant
play
please
point
pony
pretty
print
prize
problem
proud
pull
puppy
push
put

Q
question
quick
quiet

quit
quite

R
rabbit
rain
ran
reach
read
real
red
remember
ride
right
river
room
round
run

S
sad
said
same
sat
Saturday
saw
school
second
see
seem

send
sentence
seven
several
she
short
should
show
side
since
sing
sister
six
sleep
slowly
small
snow
so
some
soon
south
space
stand
start
stay
stop
store
story
street

such
suddenly
swim

T
take
talk
teach
tell
ten
than
thank
that
the
their
them
then
there
these
they
thing
think
third
this
those
thought
three
through

Thursday
time
to
today
together
told
tomorrow
too
took
toward
town
toy
travel
tree
tried
truck
true
Tuesday
turn
two

U
under
until
up
upon
us
use

usually

V
very
visit
voice

W
wait
walk
want
was
wash
watch
water
we
Wednesday
week
well
went
were
west
what
when
which
while
white
who
why

will

with

woman

word

work

world

would

write

Y

yard

year

yellow

yes

yesterday

you

young

your

TURNING WORDS INTO MENTAL IMAGES (A READING COMPREHENSION SKILL)

Converting math words into mental images. Students often have trouble doing story problems. The way to begin to help them is to have them work with very simple problems, draw pictures, and use manipulatives.

When you expose the students to Dittoes #46–49, you may want to do each activity sheet as a guided practice sheet. Go to the board and draw; students watch and draw on their sheets. Explain to the students what you are doing. By changing the numbers in each problem, you can reuse each ditto several times, having students do the same problems as independent practice. Consult regular class math workbooks at the second-grade level to find other problems. Encourage students to draw pictures.

I urge you to have students express answers using number words; it will help them become familiar with the spelling of these words.

In this section you will also find Dittoes #50 and 51. These are designed to encourage students to convert words into mental images.

Using this skill as a daily sponge activity. When the children enter the room after recess, you often need a few minutes to settle problems and/or get organized. Write a sentence on the board and ask students to draw a picture on a 1/4 sheet of paper to illustrate it. It will take them about five minutes. Quickly look at the pictures and give feedback.

DITTO #45, STUDENT NOTEBOOK HANDOUT, NUMBER WORDS

1 — ONE	11 — ELEVEN	30 — THIRTY
2 — TWO	12 — TWELVE	40 — FORTY
3 — THREE	13 — THIRTEEN	50 — FIFTY
4 — FOUR	14 — FOURTEEN	60 — SIXTY
5 — FIVE	15 — FIFTEEN	70 — SEVENTY
6 — SIX	16 — SIXTEEN	80 — EIGHTY
7 — SEVEN	17 — SEVENTEEN	90 — NINETY
8 — EIGHT	18 — EIGHTEEN	100 — HUNDRED
9 — NINE	19 — NINETEEN	1000 — THOUSAND
10 — TEN	20 — TWENTY	1,000,000 — MILLION

Name _____

DITTO #46, TURNING WORDS INTO MENTAL IMAGES
(A READING COMPREHENSION SKILL)

Directions: <u>Read</u> each problem. <u>Draw</u> a picture to show what the words mean. <u>Write</u> the answers to the problem using words. The first one is done for you.

1. Bob's mother told him to get

   out <u>five</u> flower pots.

   Then she told him to put <u>two</u>

   flowers in each pot.

   How many flowers did Bob plant ?

   <u>ten flowers</u>

- -

2. You have _____ cupcakes to share with me.

   How many cupcakes will each of us get?

   _____

- -

3. _____ children were playing.

   _____ more children came to play.

   How many children are playing now?

   _____

Name _____

DITTO #47, TURNING WORDS INTO MENTAL IMAGES
(A READING COMPREHENSION SKILL)

Directions: <u>Read</u> each problem. <u>Draw</u> a picture to show what the words mean. <u>Write</u> the answer using words.

1. I got a pack of gum.

   It had _____ sticks of gum in it.

   I ate _____ sticks and gave

   _____ to my dad.

   How many sticks of gum are left?

   _____

- -

2. Sal loves pets. She has_____

   dogs, _____ cats and _____ rabbits.

   How many pets does she have in all?

   _____

- -

3. Anna is making a garden.

   She makes _____ rows.

   She puts _____ tomato plants

   in each row.

   How many tomato plants did she plant?

   _____

Name _____

DITTO #48, TURNING WORDS INTO MENTAL IMAGES
(A READING COMPREHENSION SKILL)

Directions: <u>Read</u> each problem. <u>Draw</u> a picture to show what the words mean. <u>Write</u> the answer in words.

1. You are going to play marbles.

   You have _____ marbles to share with your friend.

   How many will each of you start with?

   _____

- -

2. Sam has _____ dimes, _____

   nickels and _____ pennies.

   How much money is that? _____

- -

3. Daddy gives you a box of candy.

   It has _____ bonbons in it.

   You give _____ to mother and

   _____ to your dad.

   How many candies are left? _____

- -

4. _____ kids are playing.

   _____ kids have to go home.

   How many kids are left? _____

Name _____

DITTO #49, TURNING WORDS INTO MENTAL IMAGES
(A READING COMPREHENSION SKILL)

Directions: <u>Read</u> each problem. <u>Draw</u> a picture to show what the words mean. <u>Write</u> the answer in words.

1. A loaf of bread has _____ slices.

   If you use two slices to make a sandwich,

   how many sandwiches can you make from

   that loaf of bread? _____

- -

2. Mother makes _____ pies.

   She cuts each pie into _____ slices.

   How many slices of pie are there in all?

   _____

- -

3. You got a dozen cookies.

   You ate _____.

   How many cookies are left? _____

- -

4. There are _____ teams,

   _____ kids on each team.

   How many kids in all? _____

Name _____

DITTO #50, TURNING WORDS INTO MENTAL IMAGES

Directions: Draw a picture to show what the words mean.

It was a hot day so I went swimming.	Two boys are playing ball.
The little girl had one finger in her mouth.	There were two eggs in the bird's nest.

DITTO #51, TURNING WORDS INTO MENTAL IMAGES

Directions: Draw a picture to show what the words mean.

A little worm is on the flower.	The boy will paint his wagon.
The cat ran up a tree to get away from the dog.	Two children looked out the window at the rain.

Other sentences you can use to have students illustrate they are converting words into mental images are listed here. When you look at the pictures, be sure the child illustrated each underlined word.

1. The <u>two children</u> were <u>making</u> a <u>snowman</u>.
2. <u>A girl and boy</u> were taking a <u>walk</u> in the <u>woods</u>.
3. <u>Father</u> is <u>reading</u> a <u>book</u> to his <u>children</u>.
4. The <u>boy</u> has a pet <u>duck</u>.
5. The <u>boy put a band-aid</u> on his <u>finger</u>.
6. The <u>boy put on</u> his <u>coat</u> and <u>hat</u>.
7. The <u>girl looked under</u> her <u>bed</u> for her <u>shoe</u>.
8. <u>Mother gave</u> the <u>boy</u> a <u>book</u> to read.
9. The <u>boy</u> is <u>raking leaves</u> into a <u>pile</u>.
10. <u>Two girls</u> are going for a <u>ride in</u> the <u>boat</u>.
11. <u>Mother picked</u> a <u>bunch of flowers</u>.
12. <u>Father</u> is out in the <u>rain mowing</u> the <u>grass</u>.
13. <u>She saw a snake</u> moving <u>in</u> the <u>tall grass</u>.
14. The <u>woman</u> is <u>walking</u> her <u>dog</u>.
15. <u>He got</u> a <u>two-scoop ice cream cone</u>.
16. The <u>baby</u> was <u>in his bed</u>.
17. The <u>girl</u> has <u>long, dark, straight hair</u>.
18. The <u>boy</u> is <u>playing with a toy car</u>.
19. <u>Mother</u> likes to <u>read in bed</u>.
20. The <u>cat</u> is <u>sitting by</u> the <u>door</u>.
21. The <u>girl</u> is <u>riding</u> her <u>bike</u>.
22. <u>Father looked at his watch</u> to see what time it was.
23. <u>Two boys</u> were <u>looking in</u> the <u>bushes</u> for their lost ball.
24. <u>Two cats</u> were having a <u>fight</u>.
25. The <u>man</u> is <u>making a dog house</u>.
26. <u>Father</u> was <u>carrying two big bags</u> of food <u>into the house</u>.
27. The <u>boy</u> is <u>washing dishes</u> and the <u>girl</u> is <u>drying them</u>.
28. The <u>boy kicked the ball</u> as hard as he could.
29. <u>Two girls</u> were <u>playing a game of checkers</u>.
30. The <u>baby</u> was <u>crying</u> because <u>his toy had fallen on the floor</u>.

ANTONYMS REVISITED

Antonyms are words that have opposite meanings, such as "good" is the opposite of "bad." Here is a list of antonyms you will find useful.

above — below	left — right	rich — poor
adult — child	long — short	right — wrong
apart — together	lost — found	
		same — different
dead — alive	many — few	small — large
dirty — clean	mine — yours	smooth — rough
	more — less	spend — save
forgot — remembered	much — little	straight — crooked
		strong — weak
gentle — mean	near — far	
get — give	noisy — quiet	tame — wild
	open — close	to — from
healthy — ill		top — bottom
heavy — light	part — whole	
	push — pull	

NOTE: You can teach these antonyms using the flash-card method described in Unit 2 of this book or you may have students complete Ditto #52.

COMPOUND WORDS

Compound words are words that have been formed by putting two smaller words together. The list you find here (Ditto #53) is not comprehensive, but will give your students an exposure to this type of words. The list includes the words your students will need to complete the activities found in this section.

Name _____

DITTO #52, ANTONYMS

DITTO #53, COMPOUND WORDS

afternoon
afterthought

airmail
airplane
airport
airtight

anybody
anyhow
anymore
anyone
anything
anywhere

backbite
backbone
backfire
background

bareback
barefoot

baseball
basketball

bathroom
bathtub

bedroom
bedspread

birthday

blackboard

bookcase

bookdrop
bookkeeper
bookmark
bookstore

breakdown
breakfast

broadcast
broadside

carpool
cardboard

classmate
classroom

clipboard

crossbones
crossroads
crosswalk

cupboard
cupcake

darkroom

daybreak
daydream
daylight
daylight

doghouse

downfall
downpour

downstairs
downtown

drawback
drawbridge
drawstring

drugstore

earthquake

everybody
everyone
everything
everywhere

firehouse
fireplace
fireside
firewood
fireworks

flashback
flashcube
flashlight

football
foothold
footnote
footstool

frostbite
fruitcake
fruitcup

gentleman

gingerale
gingerbread

goldfish
goodbye
goodnight

gumdrop

haircut
hairbrush

handbook
handcuff
handmade
handshake

headache
headboard
headlight
headline
headquarters

highchair
highland
highrise
highway

holdup

homemade
homesick
hometown
homework

horseback
horsefly

horseshoe

however

housework

indoor
inside
into

landlady
landlord
landslide

leftover

lipstick

lookout

loudspeaker

mailbox
mailman

newsboy
newscast
newspaper

nightgown

notebook
notepaper
nothing

outbreak
outcome
outdoor
outfit

outlaws
outlook
outnumber
outside
outspoken
outstanding
outward

overall
overboard
overcome
overlook
overpass
oversight
overthrow
overtook
overwork

pancake

paperback

playground
playhouse
playmate

railroad

rainbow
raincoat
raindrop
rainfall

ripoff

roadside
roadway

roommate

runway

sidewalk

shoelace

skateboard

softball

something

spotlight

sunflower
sunlight
sunrise
sunset
sunshine

stairway

storehouse

textbook

tidepool

tiptoe

toothache
toothbrush
toothpaste

turnoff

underground
undertaker

uprise
uproot
upset
upstairs
uptown

walkway

waterfall
waterfront
watermelon

weekday
weekend

whirlpool

wristwatch

DITTO #54, MAKING COMPOUND WORDS

Directions for Teacher: Cut out the following words. Mark the back of each word card with an *A*. Place the words in an envelope marked *A*. When the words are given to a student, model how the word pieces may be combined to form compound words.

any	over	every	look
in	where	mail	chair
man	some	thing	out
side	gentle	no	way
door	laws	one	high

Possible solutions include:

anywhere	everywhere	somewhere	nothing	lookout
anything	everyone	someone	outlaws	outside
anyway	everything	something	outlook	mailman
overlook	highway	chairman	inside	
outdoor	highchair	gentleman	indoor	

If the student offers another solution, check the accuracy of his or her offering with a dictionary.

DITTO #55, MAKING COMPOUND WORDS

Directions for Teacher: Cut out the following words. Mark the back of each word card with a *B*. Place the words in an envelope marked *B*. When the words are given to a student, model how the word pieces may be combined to form compound words.

up	down	drop	foot
hold	stairs	bare	gum
coat	note	over	book
town	all	ball	home
come	made	rain	work

Possible solutions include:

upstairs	footnote	raincoat	bookdrop	homemade
downstairs	football	overcoat	notebook	homework
uptown	foothold	overbook	gumdrop	hometown
raindrop	barefoot	overcome	overwork	overall

If the student offers another solution, check the accuracy of his or her offering with a dictionary.

DITTO #56, MAKING COMPOUND WORDS

Directions for Teacher: Cut out the following words. Mark the back of each word card with a *C*. Place the words in an envelope marked *C*. When the words are given to a student, model how the word pieces may be combined to form compound words.

car	pool	whirl	pan
cake	roar	fruit	post
black	board	cup	tide
skate	head	rip	set
up	sun	rise	root

Possible solutions include:

carpool	cardboard	fruitcake	cupcake	fruitcup
tidepool	blackboard	pancake	sunset	sunrise
whirlpool	skateboard	uprise	uproot	postcard
riptide	headboard	blackhead	upset	

If the student offers another solution, check the accuracy of his or her offering with a dictionary.

DITTO #57, MAKING COMPOUND WORDS

Directions for Teacher: Cut out the following words. Mark the back of each word card with a *D*. Place the words in an envelope marked *D*. When the words are given to a student, model how the word pieces may be combined to form compound words.

water	hand	fall	front
light	melon	book	cuff
quarters	shake	head	line
ache	rain	tooth	bow
brush	hair	paste	cut

Possible solutions include:

watermelon	handbook	headache	haircut	rainfall
waterfront	handcuff	headline	hairbrush	rainbow
waterfall	handshake	headquarters	headlight	
toothache	toothpaste	toothbrush		

If the student offers another solution, check his or her offering with a dictionary.

Teaching Students How to Recognize Questions

One of the more difficult things for LD students to grasp is when to use a period and when to use a question mark. When I began teaching, I tried to explain that if someone says something to you that requires you to answer, *that is a question.* If someone says something that does not make you want to answer, *that is a sentence and it needs a period.* It sounds simple enough, but the students didn't get it! So I tried something different. I posted the sheet "Words That Signal Questions" (Ditto #58) on the door and every morning, for three weeks, we named the words. After going over the words chorally, the students looked at five sentences and punctuated them (see Dittoes #59 and 60). They got it! At the end of three weeks they were pretty good at recognizing questions.

You can write additional activities for as many days you think they are needed. If you use sentences that contain only words on the "500 Most Used Words" List, the activity can give reading practice. Even students who are virtual nonreaders can learn to consult the chart and punctuate accordingly.

The last week, novelty was a component of the oral activity—we added sound when we reviewed the dittoes. A student would read his or her answer to the class: if the answer was a period, a "splatting noise" was made with the mouth; if the answer was a question, a noise that slid from a high pitch to a lower pitch was made.

Contractions

In the course of speaking and writing, we are prone to take shortcuts by combining two words in a shortened version. The list you find on Ditto #61 contains most but not all of these combinations. There are a few less commonly used ones that have been omitted.

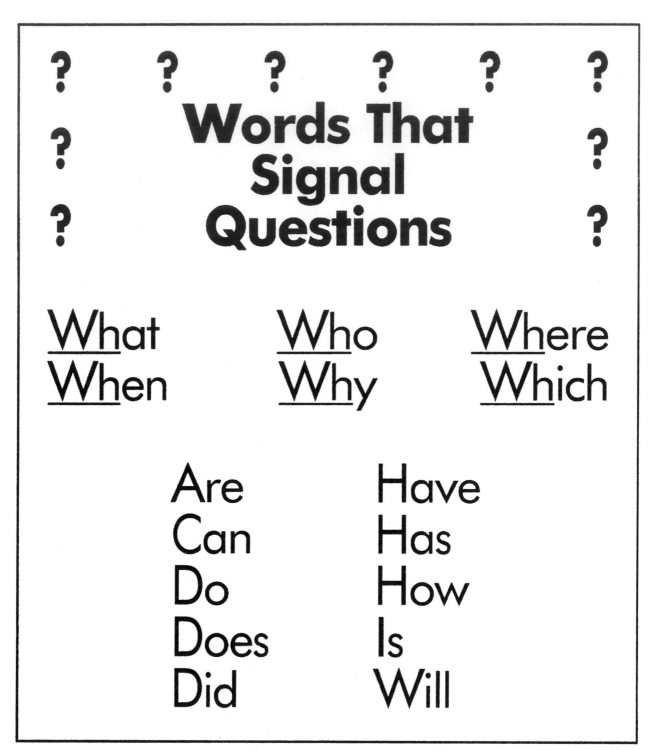

? ? ? ? ? ?

? ?

? ?

Words That Signal Questions

<u>Wh</u>at <u>Wh</u>o <u>Wh</u>ere
<u>Wh</u>en <u>Wh</u>y <u>Wh</u>ich

Are Have
Can Has
Do How
Does Is
Did Will

Name _____

DITTO #59, HOW TO RECOGNIZE QUESTIONS

Directions:

1. <u>Underline</u> the first word of each sentence.
2. <u>Look at the chart</u> of the words that signal questions.
3. Is that underlined word on the chart? If the answer is <u>yes</u>, put a question mark (?) at the end of the sentence. If the answer is <u>no</u>, put a period (.) at the end of the sentence.

- What time does your plane leave ____
- Why are you always late ____
- My bed needs to be made ____
- Is the dog outside ____
- The nurse gave me a shot ____

- Did you see which way he went ____
- I want to go with Mother to the store ____
- Have you told her you can't come to her party ____
- May I use your book ____
- How did you get the answer to that question ____

- They took a walk in the park ____
- Where did Father go ____
- Will you help me clean my room ____
- She does not like that kind of pie ____
- Can you wink one eye at a time ____

Name _____

DITTO #60, HOW TO RECOGNIZE QUESTIONS

Directions:

1. <u>Underline</u> the first word of each sentence.
2. <u>Look at the chart</u> of words that signal questions.
3. Is that underlined word on the chart? If the answer is <u>yes</u>, put a question mark (?) at the end of the sentence. If the answer is <u>no</u>, put a period (.) at the end of the sentence.

- Would you like to play checkers ____
- What kind of dog is that ____
- Are you having fun ____
- Next week we are going to the beach ____
- Has she ever been to New York ____

- Who is that girl over there ____
- Mother said I had to come home before dark ____
- He said he would help me with my math ____
- Will it rain today ____
- Does your dad work on Saturdays ____

- Can you ride a one-wheeled bike ____
- Is that your cat up in the tree ____
- How many people did you ask to your party ____
- Why does she call you Tom when your name is Thomas ____
- What did you do with my book ____

DITTO #61, STUDENT NOTEBOOK HANDOUT, CONTRACTIONS

I am = I'm

I have = I've

I will = I'll

I would = I'd

you are = you're

you have = you've

you will = you'll

you would = you'd

he is = he's

he will = he'll

he would = he'd

she is = she's

she will = she'll

she would = she'd

it is = it's

it will = it'll

we are = we're

we have = we've

we will = we'll

we would = we'd

they are = they're

they have = they've

they will = they'll

they would = they'd

here is = here's

that is = that's

there is = there's

what is = what's

who will = who'll

could have = could've

should have = should've

would have = would've

might have = might've

are not = aren't

can not = can't

did not = didn't

do not = don't

does not = doesn't

had not = hadn't

has not = hasn't

have not = haven't

is not = isn't

could not = couldn't

should not = shouldn't

would not = won't

Name _____

DITTO #62, CONTRACTIONS

Directions: <u>Read</u> each sentence. <u>Rewrite</u> the sentence using the contraction for each under-lined word. The first sentence is done for you. After doing the ditto, read all sentences aloud so you can hear how the use of the contractions makes the sentence flow more easily.

1. <u>I am</u> going to have a birthday next week.

   <u>I'm going to have a birthday next week.</u>

2. <u>I will</u> ask about twenty friends to my party.

   _____

   _____

3. <u>You are</u> going to come, <u>are not</u> you?

   _____

   _____

4. <u>We will</u> play games and then <u>there will</u> be ice cream.

   _____

   _____

5. I love to play Pin-the-Tail-on-the-Donkey, <u>do not</u> you?

   _____

   _____

6. Best of all, <u>there is</u> a pile of gifts to open.

   _____

   _____

Name _____

DITTO #63, CONTRACTIONS

Directions: <u>Read</u> each sentence. <u>Rewrite</u> the sentence using the contraction for each under-lined word. The first sentence is done for you. After doing the ditto, read all sentences aloud so you can hear how the use of the contractions makes the sentence flow more easily.

1. Next week, <u>we are</u> going to visit my aunt and uncle.

   <u>Next week, we're going to visit my aunt and uncle.</u> _____

2. I like him but <u>she is</u> an old busy body.

   _____

   _____

3. I <u>would not</u> go if my mother <u>did not</u> make me.

   _____

   _____

4. Aunt Martha will say, "<u>Do not</u> touch that! You <u>should not</u> when you have food in your mouth! <u>Can not</u> you sit still?"

   _____

   _____

5. Next thing you know, <u>she will</u> make my mom cry.

   _____

   _____

6. My uncle is nice. <u>He will</u> let me ride his horse.

   _____

   _____

One More Suggestion for Teaching Contractions

You would think students would see the difference in the words "is not" and "isn't" but they don't. They can do the dittoes and never understand that when you condense the two words, you have omitted some letters and in their place put an apostrophe to indicate you left out some letters.

Put some of the contractions on the board and ask various students to come and circle the letters that were left out and explain what the apostrophe means. For example:

can not can't	Even though you have just explained to them that some letters have been left out, the child may not be able to see that two letters were omitted. So explain again.
she would she'd	This time you have omitted four letters. Will the students be able to circle the correct letters?

This is a board activity you may have to do several days using and reusing words from the list until students become proficient at the skill and familiar with the contractions.

WRITING STORIES IN THEIR OWN WORDS

At this point students can be encouraged to listen to and rewrite familiar stories in their own words (utilizing the "500 Most Used Words" List).

They seem to enjoy rewriting stories they have heard read multiple times, such as "Little Red Riding Hood," "The Three Little Pigs," "Goldilocks and the Three Bears," or "King Midas and the Golden Touch." If students have had sufficient experiences, they usually can do this; if they have only heard the story once, they can't, so you have to find out what they have read and determined if they can tell it orally before asking them to write it.

Some kids will get so carried away that they want to write the entire story in one day! In my experience, however, I found it was best to have students work on this project for 20 minutes each day until they were finished. A benefit of the 20-minute limit was that I looked at their books every night. Errors in syntax were caught and fixed before there was too much to recopy. If I circled a word, this meant they had misspelled it and that it was a word they could find on the "500 Most Used Words" List. At the beginning of each writing period, therefore, they made corrections and reread what they wrote the day before (sometimes to me, sometimes to the class, sometimes to their partner); then they went on to add to their story. Students who finished their stories first helped others. Stories were illustrated, laminated, and made into classroom books to be enjoyed by others.

MATERIALS FOR STUDENTS
FUNCTIONING
AT LEVEL 2.5 TO 2.9

OBJECTIVES FOR LEVEL 2.5 TO 2.9

- Given two lists of six words with different first letters, _____ will be able to correctly alphabetize the words.

- After using the 40 sets of practice sheets, the student will take the posttest for Decoding Set A. _____ will say the words with 80% accuracy.

- After a portion of text is read to the student, _____ will be able to make sensible predictions (five out of five trials).

- After reading a factual passage of about 200 to 250 words, _____ will be able to write five self-testing-type questions.

- Shown 20 flash cards (ten nouns, ten verbs), _____ will be able to classify the words as to whether they are nouns or verbs.

- _____ will orally read aloud to an adult for 15 minutes each day, receiving immediate feedback on any words missed.

- When given five nouns, _____ will write a sentence for each. (Each sentence will begin with a capital letter and end with a period or question mark; will be at least four words long; will contain a subject noun, verb, and phrase. These standards will be told to the student before the student starts the activity.)

Student's Reminder for Decoding and How to Use It

The purpose of the decoding lessons found in this section is to help the student fine-tune his or her ability to work out unknown words. If thoroughly taught the exercises in this section alone can increase a student's reading speed and prowess by a full grade level or more.

The materials found in this section *presume* that the student can:

1. give the correct sound for all alphabet letters
2. understand that vowels have two sounds (recognize common vowel patterns, have some preliminary knowledge of the one-vowel/two-vowel rules explained in Chapter 11 of Volume I)
3. be familiar with special combinations
4. blend letters into words

If the student *cannot* do all these things, go back to the previous units and teach all of these skills before attempting to teach this material. If you did attempt to teach these lessons without the student being ready, you would only convince the student that he or she is stupid and that reading is too hard. The ditto activities in this section are not appropriate for students with severe weaknesses in decoding; but if the student is solidly at level 2.5, then he or she can really add to his or her self confidence and build power in decoding.

Begin by giving the pretest found on Ditto #65. **"I'm going to see how well you can read words. Take your time to look at the word and to think about it. If you blurt something out and it is wrong, I must record it as a miss even if you get the word right on a second try—so be careful. I do not expect you to get all the words right, but I do want to see what you already know."**

Most LD children will score around 40% on the pretest. If they score less, you will know you need to teach what was presented in earlier units of this book.

You can expect students who participate in all daily lessons and do all 40 dittoes one-to-one with the teacher or aide (with immediate feedback when errors are made) to make between 80% and 100% when the posttest is given. This pretest/posttest sampling of the same words is very convincing data that the student has learned something from you and makes an excellent portfolio entry.

At the end of the pretest, explain to the student what his or her score was and how you are going to help him or her improve it dramatically.

Give the student a copy of the "Student's Reminder for Decoding" (Ditto #64) to place in his or her notebook. You also need to display the vowel sound bulletin board (see Chapter 11 in Volume I; you will find the materials for the bulletin board in Unit 2 of this book).

Each day go over with all the students the sounds of the short and long vowels. Stand at the bulletin board and point to the <u>a</u>. Say: **"What does this letter sound like?"** The students make the sound heard at the beginning of apple. Be certain they are not saying apple. Then say: **"<u>A</u> can also say <u>a</u>** (tell them the long sound). **What letters usually make the <u>a</u> say "a"?** Have them read and repeat patterns. Show several examples of words with these patterns, emphasizing the long sound of the <u>a</u>. Do the same with each of the vowels, talking about the short and long sounds.

Next, go down the "Student's Reminder for Decoding," saying: **"What does <u>sh</u> sound like?"** Give the sound for the students to repeat. Do this with each letter on the Reminder.

After a week of this review, talk about Rules 1, 2, and 3, and give examples. Show the students how to apply the rules to given words. Use the Resource Word Lists from Unit 3 to help. Do this daily for five days.

During week 3, pull students aside in pairs or groups of three and lead them through the process of marking a worksheet. First have them go down the 20 words and put a small v under every vowel. Next, have them look for the vc/cv pattern and put a slash on the paper to show where each word syllabicates. Finally, have the students put a long mark over the long vowels only. (Any vowel that does not say its name will carry the short sound.) Go down the list round robin, each student giving a word and explaining to the others how the word is worked out. Students cannot just get by because they happened to "know" it. They must explain each part of the word to the others. If a child cannot work a word out, you will give help. If you must give a student help with every word, it either means the student is not ready for this activity or is not giving it his or her best effort. You may need to review the whole sheet with him or her later in the day. Sometimes a student will do considerably better when being seen alone.

After a week, you can give out the ditto, let students mark it alone and, when they say they are ready to tell you all the words, you listen to them, give feedback on any word missed and record their daily score. At the end of the ditto session, you can go word for word through the list, letting students explain to others why a given word does what it does.

When you decide to teach this skill, it is extremely important to do it daily. The constant attention to the skill is necessary to get results.

Student's Reminder for Decoding

Rule 1: Count the vowels.

If there is one: a = (apple) as in apple e = edge i = itch

o = (octopus) as in octopus u = up as in up

Rule 2: Watch for vc/cv and vc/ccv.

If there is, the word breaks into syllables. Example: bet/ter

vccv

Otherwise, bē cāme

Rule 3: Watch for combinations.

sh =	er ⎫ as in	wr = wr
ch = or k	ir ⎬ her	kn = kn
th =	ur ⎭ girl	gh = ghost
ph = f	burn	night
	or = as in for	laugh (f)
	ar = as in car	
oo = as in too	al = all	c = k
ing = thing	oi/oy = as in	ce ⎫
ou = out	boy or oil	ci ⎬ says
		cy ⎭ s
ow ⎰ as in now	au/aw = saw	g = go
⎱ or snōw		
tion/sion = shun	y = yes	ge ⎫ may
	my (ī)	gi ⎬ say
	happy (ē)	gy ⎭ j

Name _____

Pretest date _____ score _____

Posttest date _____ score _____

DITTO #65, SET A: DECODING PRETEST/POSTTEST

Directions: Student is given up to 30 seconds to name each word. Each correct response is worth 5%. The child's first response is the one recorded, even if the student self-corrects.

matter	**crowd**	**knight**	**mop**
story	**ridden**	**wore**	**lesson**
bacon	**spoon**	**lap**	**rug**
belly	**lather**	**rice**	**wrench**
charming	**turtle**	**jail**	**dawdle**

alone	painter	doll	brown
circus	flower	city	balloon
shut	birthday	coat	spring
fling	raccoon	each	became
chip	road	soft	roof

name _____ score _____ date _____ Set A—Lesson 1

shark	tractor	marsh	subway
clown	peanut	goat	butter
duck	branch	camp	lift
count	faster	sang	shiny
uncle	circle	into	cigar

name _____ score _____ date _____ Set A—Lesson 2

DITTO #67, DECODING—SET A

large	surprise	tease	beside
tail	bottle	lake	sound
snake	bridge	swing	gate
block	really	mail	sheep
round	whisper	little	wish

name _____ score _____ date _____ Set A—Lesson 3

board	mettle	bush	king
clock	buckle	warm	alarm
boast	silver	sock	beginning
ankle	certain	art	captain
shave	amuse	moon	cellar

name _____ score _____ date _____ Set A—Lesson 4

bottom	careful	brave	corn
candy	dollar	farther	fence
flash	glass	gold	hunter
later	line	knock	mouth
rock	center	pile	ship

name _____ score _____ date _____ Set A—Lesson 5

cream	broken	grouch	burn
flour	dinner	rope	grin
south	happen	lot	lucky
horn	chin	pair	corner
turn	hide	lock	proud

name _____ score _____ date _____ Set A—Lesson 6

bone	chicken	church	hound
card	found	splash	row
rest	silly	window	refuse
sled	throw	reach	share
root	ranch	best	rest

name _____ score _____ date _____ Set A—Lesson 7

test	cheer	beach	still
stick	summer	west	lick
borrow	grow	cheese	winter
rattle	tooth	cozy	loose
dirty	clap	dip	lady

name _____ score _____ date _____ Set A—Lesson 8

smile	blossom	contest	allow
charge	trip	arrow	aim
smell	blade	cheer	bug
breeze	awful	nest	paw
nibble	danger	decide	fear

name _____ score _____ date _____ Set A—Lesson 9

storm	chain	porch	bubble
jaw	arrive	saw	star
cloth	coast	awake	reply
spy	battle	lower	oil
broil	excuse	desk	exercise

name _____ score _____ date _____ Set A—Lesson 10

DITTO #71, DECODING—SET A

strange	tiny	strong	smart
bunch	straw	bead	toil
crawl	arm	offer	escape
soil	announce	boot	brush
cheap	cloud	blow	right

name _____ score _____ date _____ Set A—Lesson 11

sorry	dish	stuck	teach
base	tired	bent	harm
draw	point	shawl	join
night	broom	fight	dime
exit	dried	cost	discover

name _____ score _____ date _____ Set A—Lesson 12

dawn	chatter	chance	carve
shirt	voice	shot	jacket
pool	delight	coward	fellow
bucket	foolish	guard	heel
hose	hollow	knife	known

name _____ score _____ date _____ Set A—Lesson 13

chest	shine	inch	class
grab	choice	tool	depend
tight	frown	might	history
gaze	pocket	hoop	jar
keeper	husband	sheet	hospital

name _____ score _____ date _____ Set A—Lesson 14

DITTO #73, DECODING—SET A

shape	narrow	doctor	sharp
coil	coach	east	mistake
enter	neither	order	ripe
rooster	slide	rush	strike
wrap	rich	pocket	wrong

name _____ score _____ date _____ Set A—Lesson 15

cool	patch	remain	rubber
stuff	sweep	swallow	wisdom
wreck	mark	wrist	toss
stream	shore	stretch	chill
wing	ugly	spoil	family

name _____ score _____ date _____ Set A—Lesson 16

DITTO #74, DECODING—SET A

market	shoot	smoke	bring
snap	only	sale	finally
shelf	trot	needle	throat
handle	price	lumber	meal
path	route	plain	moan

name _____ score _____ date _____ Set A—Lesson 17

safe	batter	bowl	bundle
useful	crash	cattle	carpet
content	drove	example	fed
club	force	fresh	greedy
gather	sour	expel	list

name _____ score _____ date _____ Set A—Lesson 18

DITTO #75, DECODING—SET A

rescue	wring	unite	softly
saving	peddler	mice	match
tunnel	shake	drool	thirsty
bath	lonely	note	pretend
nickel	intend	penny	lap

name _____ score _____ date _____ Set A—Lesson 19

lively	chose	lovely	speed
drift	shade	brick	crowd
event	hidden	harbor	finger
torch	nod	plate	ribbon
soap	thick	team	thousand

name _____ score _____ date _____ Set A—Lesson 20

blame	knelt	tribe	tent
spent	shame	twenty	spider
trousers	sigh	lump	jelly
single	rug	slice	thirty
lying	stage	explain	complain

name _____ score _____ date _____ Set A—Lesson 21

tame	rent	forty	belt
plenty	melt	twice	mayor
sweet	hug	master	hungry
juice	polite	frame	job
angry	scour	sent	clear

name _____ score _____ date _____ Set A—Lesson 22

DITTO #77, DECODING—SET A

glance	swap	suppose	hang
fail	bounce	set	leash
purple	flicking	ground	hole
tossing	taken	scooter	worth
cruise	power	capsule	reason

name _____ score _____ date _____ Set A—Lesson 23

surface	really	else	string
leap	brass	challenge	terrible
trait	stuck	absolute	crisis
watch	frog	edge	shop
drown	huge	motor	coffee

name _____ score _____ date _____ Set A—Lesson 24

DITTO #78, DECODING—SET A

shout	garden	excite	seat
dine	maple	lawn	sample
globe	donkey	about	close
scare	serve	bitter	shirt
chair	ruin	relax	enormous

name _____ score _____ date _____ Set A—Lesson 25

convince	nature	sternly	future
drop	scout	distant	meekly
stage	message	shy	produce
nectar	joke	sting	blaring
contain	ladder	easily	coax

name _____ score _____ date _____ Set A—Lesson 26

DITTO #79, DECODING—SET A

fifty	mixture	rose	claw
raw	simple	result	puzzle
deal	churn	led	knot
sun	success	town	tame
pitch	quilt	fixture	sorrow

name _____ score _____ date _____Set A—Lesson 27

approach	bright	folding	pie
dream	sink	swept	chore
pink	budge	bride	groom
pardon	moment	evening	brain
scout	went	hard	sprout

name _____ score _____ date _____Set A—Lesson 28

DITTO #80, DECODING—SET A

swell	part	monster	temper
invite	grocery	hurry	people
pounding	adventure	lodge	silently
layer	born	surround	cotton
grunted	pinch	nasty	person

name _____ score _____ date _____ Set A—Lesson 29

dream	blanket	faint	mountain
wobbly	wonder	sister	wipe
speak	munching	yummy	basket
barber	comforting	manage	upon
scissors	giant	slurp	since

name _____ score _____ date _____ Set A—Lesson 30

© 1995 by The Center for Applied Research in Education

DITTO #81, DECODING—SET A

beneath	brush	stand	wedge
clump	hammer	dough	graze
thought	gently	trail	curve
loom	straight	except	trial
carton	plastic	cage	whiskers

name _____ score _____ date _____ Set A—Lesson 31

bought	nearly	dairy	pencil
diary	hiding	easy	hamster
cartoon	size	slippery	punch
poking	stirring	swoop	trash
waddle	cabbage	squeeze	square

name _____ score _____ date _____ Set A—Lesson 32

settle	distance	scold	tied
securely	prepare	wander	flying
pace	darted	fought	tangle
fountain	scramble	direction	month
connection	ostrich	frighten	vacation

name _____ score _____ date _____ Set A—Lesson 33

creature	brittle	furniture	bench
curtains	gazing	burrow	fever
basement	mood	arguing	snowy
resist	silence	department	witch
shelter	quite	curl	disappear

name _____ score _____ date _____ Set A—Lesson 34

DITTO #83, DECODING—SET A

poor	slender	middle	wrath
package	attic	deserted	blur
commanded	glide	staring	ledge
valley	stone	battle	bruise
joust	gallop	tending	field

name _____ score _____ date _____Set A—Lesson 35

smooth	wrong	execute	chief
brief	garbage	moist	yarn
jungle	bothering	check	extend
latch	stolen	whimper	advice
excellent	complete	fiber	introduce

name _____ score _____ date _____ Set A—Lesson 36

DITTO #84, DECODING—SET A

niece	wrote	expert	haul
orchard	relief	sapling	owner
caught	station	crunch	collar
nation	admire	taught	fatal
recite	eraser	struggle	cottage

name _____ score _____ date _____ Set A—Lesson 37

piece	harvest	scarf	believe
aroma	author	chug	sorting
because	twisted	leap	autumn
flame	naughty	loop	scatter
cart	payment	motion	change

name _____ score _____ date _____ Set A—Lesson 38

chat	weakly	lend	cereal
boom	glitter	judge	innocent
across	sticker	dusty	sight
trudge	straw	crept	bound
giggling	awkward	perform	question

name _____ score _____ date _____ Set A—Lesson 39

rage	guide	icy	stumble
spark	fond	rare	suggestion
inform	interrupt	grain	scorching
towel	awning	floppy	huddle
attention	harmony	request	flaw

name _____ score _____ date _____ Set A—Lesson 40

Encouraging LD Students to Become Active Readers

Good readers have active minds that are constantly interacting with the print. They are forming mental images and making predictions about what will happen next as they go along. If they receive new information as they read the story, they make adjustments in the mental pictures that have formed. After a good reader completes something, he or she often does some self-questioning to satisfy him- or herself that he or she really understood the action of the story or got the information provided. Research has shown that LD students do not do these things routinely, so we have to try to stimulate them to develop these skills.

You will find three types of activities to encourage students to become more interactive with the text:

1. Revisit "Turning Words into Mental Images" (see Unit 3).

2. Ask students to read some short passages and *predict* from the information given *what will happen next* (Dittoes 86-93).

3. Ask them to read some essays and write their own test questions. This is their introduction into the self-questioning technique. It also will allow you to have them review the "How to Recognize Questions" section they studied in Unit 3.

After covering these three topics, incorporate them in the students' future reading by having the students draw pictures to illustrate portions of a story, make predictions about the next page of a story before they have read it, and write their own questions and answer them.

DITTO #86, TURNING WORDS INTO MENTAL IMAGES (REVISITED), VISUALIZATION ACTIVITY

Making Cookies

On Saturday, it was raining and I was bored so Mom said I could help her make the holiday cookies. She made the dough but I did the rest.

First, I cut out four stars. I sprinkled them with brown sugar. Next, I cut out six trees. I used the round red and green coated candies to decorate them. Then, I made five crescent-shaped cookies. Finally, I made two big cookies in the shape of snowmen, using raisins for their eyes, mouths and buttons. After they were cooked I dusted them with white powdered sugar because it looks like snow.

Draw a picture below to show the cookies. Color it. You may ask your teacher what "crescent" means.

DITTO #87, TURNING WORDS INTO MENTAL IMAGES (REVISITED), VISUALIZATION ACTIVITY

The Extraterrestrial

My friend is a nut. He's always told tall tales but this week he really outdid himself. He says he was captured by an extraterrestrial creature and taken for a ride on its ship.

While he was asleep, this creature sneaked up on him and gave him some kind of shot that made him unable to talk or resist. When he opened his eyes, he saw this weird-shaped being that had three eyes, one of which was in the middle of its forehead. It lifted my friend up with its eight arms and gently carried him out to its spaceship, which was parked right there in front of the house. How absurd!

My friend said he was fascinated by the creature's pale purple skin and large round mouth that was shaped like an O. All the while they flew around, the creature hummed the same little tune. After a bit, the being returned him unharmed to his house and bed.

Draw below what you think the creature looked like. You may add any details you wish, but you must include the features given in the story.

DITTO #88, TURNING WORDS INTO MENTAL IMAGES (REVISITED), VISUALIZATION ACTIVITY

My Neighborhood

I live in a small white house that is located exactly halfway up the side of a hill. When it's time to go to school, I pick up my friend who lives in the big house next door and we trudge up to the top of the hill where the school sits on a flat mesa. When my mom runs out of something, I get sent to the store which is at the bottom of the hill. I always take our wagon. The wagon makes going down the hill a blast and it is of help when bringing the sacks back up.

Draw a picture below that shows all the details mentioned in the paragraph. You may either show me on the way to the store or on the way home. Ask your teacher to explain the word "mesa."

DITTO #89, TURNING WORDS INTO MENTAL IMAGES (REVISITED), VISUALIZATION ACTIVITY

A Birthday Party

Yesterday, I went to the best party I've ever been to. We had so much fun.

When I first walked in the door, I thought, "Ho Hum." It looked like it was going to be just your run-of-the-mill party. The house was decorated with the usual streamers and balloons and there was that game "Pin the Tail on the Donkey" on the wall. But that's where the usual jazz stopped.

We each got to choose a balloon. Then we were given paints and were told we were to paint faces on them. There were prizes for the cutest face and the ugliest face. I won one of the prizes.

As we finished the balloons, we were given little cakes to decorate. There were dishes of frosting, nuts, cherries, and small figures we could use. It was really fun.

Draw a picture below to go with this story. Try to include as many details as you can. Color it. Underline all the detail words in the story that you tried to put in your picture.

DITTO #90, TURNING WORDS INTO MENTAL IMAGES (REVISITED), VISUALIZATION ACTIVITY

The Tree House

My friends, Brian and Justin, helped me build a tree house in our big oak tree.

My Dad insisted that we build it on the lowest branch so that if anyone fell out, they would not be killed. It is about twelve feet off the ground. To get up to it, we nailed small boards to the trunk of the tree about a foot apart. These serve as steps.

Today we decided to make a dog elevator so my dog can come up. It consists of a rope with a large bucket tied to it. We throw the rope over a limb, holding one end, of course, and lower the bucket to the ground. Someone puts the dog in the bucket. As we pull down on the rope, the bucket comes up.

Draw a picture below that illustrates what the words mean. Be sure to include as many details as you can. Reread the selection and underline each detail you showed in your picture.

DITTO #91, TURNING WORDS INTO MENTAL IMAGES (REVISITED), VISUALIZATION ACTIVITY

Going to the Beach

The Jones family goes to the beach every chance they get. Mr. Jones loves to fly kites and there is almost always a nice breeze so he can get his biggest and most colorful kite up. Mrs. Jones likes to sit in her beach chair and soak up the sunshine. The twins, Tommy and Timmy, enjoy taking turns burying each other in the sand until the only part of their body still seen is the head. They have a huge beach umbrella they set up and little Amber, who is only two, likes to sit under it and scoop up sand with her shovel and put the sand into her pail. Every one enjoys the day.

Draw a picture below of the Jones family at the beach. Reread the selection and try to include as many details as you can. Go back and underline each detail you did show.

DITTO #92, TURNING WORDS INTO MENTAL IMAGES (REVISITED), VISUALIZATION ACTIVITY

Getting Things Organized

Jason had just finished rearranging the things on his bookshelves. There were actually three fairly long shelves. On the left side of the top one, he put his old stuffed Teddy Bear. Next to it he put the model car he had built last year. On the right side was his TV.

The middle shelf contained all his books held up by a really heavy pair of bookends.

On the bottom shelf, he lined up his shoes. On the left he put his hiking boots. Next to those were two pairs of sneakers and then his house shoes. Finally, he put his globe on the right side.

Draw a picture below that shows you understand what the words mean. Be careful to note each detail given.

DITTO #93, TURNING WORDS INTO MENTAL IMAGES (REVISITED), VISUALIZATION ACTIVITY

The Playground

Mrs. Brown works at a playground. She watches the children who come there and tries to see that they have a safe stay. Today, she has twelve charges. Two children are bouncing a ball back and forth between them. Three children are swinging. One child is on the slide. Two girls are playing tether ball. One little boy is sitting under the tree all by himself. The rest of the children are playing in the sandbox.

Draw a picture below that shows you understand what the words mean. Be careful to illustrate each detail.

DITTO #94, GUIDED PRACTICE—USING INFERENTIAL THINKING TO MAKE PREDICTIONS

Directions for Teacher: Do the first ditto as a group. Accept any reasonable answer. Where there arc several reasonable answers offered, ask students how they reached the conclusions.

Directions: <u>Read</u> each passage. <u>Think</u> about what it is trying to tell you. <u>Predict</u> what will happen next.

Mother has been working in her garden. It is a hot day and she begins to sweat. When she comes in, Dad says, "Your face is dirty and you don't smell like a rose."
What will happen next?

_____

_____

Little Mary is very tired. She has played hard all day. Daddy sits down to read her a story. She begins to rub her eyes and yawn.
What will happen next?

_____

_____

Daddy is painting. Little Sue is watching him.
Mother calls, "Time to eat." Dad goes into the kitchen to have his lunch.
What will happen next?

_____

_____

DITTO #95

Directions: <u>Read</u> each passage. <u>Think</u> about what it is trying to tell you. <u>Predict</u> what will happen next.

Ann rolls over to look at her clock. 7:30 A.M. "Oh great! I'm going to be late for school." She jumps out of bed and starts to dress, but she is so sleepy and tired she cannot think very well. All at once it hits her—"Today is Saturday!"

What will happen next?

_____

_____

Card 1: Using Inferential Thinking to Make Predictions

Sara and her mother are walking past the pet store. They stop to look in the windows. In one window are kittens and in the other are puppies. "They're so cute. See that fuzzy brown one?" Sara asks. "He's a darling!" Mother agrees.

What will happen next?

_____\

_____

Card 2: Using Inferential Thinking to Make Predictions

Jack's mother's birthday is tomorrow. He wants to get her a present, but he does not have any money. When his mom comes home from work, Jack sees that her car is very dirty. Suddenly he has an idea.

What will happen next?

_____

_____

Card 3: Using Inferential Thinking to Make Predictions

Name _____

DITTO #96

Directions: <u>Read</u> each passage. <u>Think</u> about what it is trying to tell you. <u>Predict</u> what will happen next.

Mr. Jones is trying to nail a new board to his fence, but it keeps falling down. He needs three hands—one to hold the nail, one to hold the board, and one to pound the hammer.

Just then the postman comes with the mail.

What will happen next?

_____

_____

Card 4: Using Inferential Thinking to Make Predictions

A huge deer stands in the meadow nibbling on tall grass. A hunter creeps quietly along trying to get as close as he can to the deer. He raises his gun to aim. A bird lets out a loud squawk.

What will happen next?

_____

_____

Card 5: Using Inferential Thinking to Make Predictions

Mother tells Jim he needs to clean his room. He keeps on playing so she tells him again. Still he does not move.

Dad tells Jim to clean his room. Jim says, "I won't do it and you can't make me!"

What will happen next?

_____

_____

Card 6: Using Inferential Thinking to Make Predictions

Name _____

DITTO #97

Directions: <u>Read</u> each passage. <u>Think</u> about what it is trying to tell you. <u>Predict</u> what will happen next.

Mrs. Green looks out in the backyard. She cannot see her dog. She goes to the door and calls but he does not come. She goes out to look around. Then she sees a hole under the fence.

What will happen next?

_____

_____

Card 7: Using Inferential Thinking to Make Predictions

The classroom is hot. Jon is bored. He leans back in his chair. The chair legs come off the floor. Suddenly Jon feels like his world is turning upside down. When he looks up, he is looking at the ceiling.

What will happen next?

_____

_____

Card 8: Using Inferential Thinking to Make Predictions

Lad is a nice dog. He lives with two cats and they are the best of friends. One day while he is in the field with Joey, a small black and white animal walks by. Lad runs right up to it. Joey yells, "No, Lad! It's a skunk!"

What will happen next?

_____

_____

Card 9: Using Inferential Thinking to Make Predictions

DITTO #98, WRITING YOUR OWN TEST QUESTIONS

Directions: Write five questions to go with this selection. Use another sheet of paper.

Time

Mothers all over the world say to their children, "Don't be late to school." Once they get to school, the kids learn that at a certain time they can go to lunch or recess. Grownups also have times to start work, to go to lunch, and to go home. Clocks and calendars are devices we all rely upon to tell time. But how did we get them?

Thousands of years ago, people realized that there was a regular order to the Earth. It got light and they called it daytime. It got dark and they called it night. They found there was a sequence to the seasons. About seven hundred years ago they realized that the way the Earth related to the sun determined when the lightness and darkness came and how the seasons changed. They made calendars and a kind of clock called a sundial.

They watched how the Earth, sun, moon, and stars moved. Soon they knew that a year is the length of time that it takes the Earth to go around the sun one time—365 days. A "moonth" (month) is the amount of time it takes the moon to go around the Earth—about 30 days.

Finally, they realized that the seasons were caused by the distance from a particular place on Earth to the sun. When the distance is the shortest, that place is having summer. When it is the farthest, that place is having winter.

DITTO #99, WRITING YOUR OWN TEST QUESTIONS

Directions: Write five questions to go with this selection. Use another sheet of paper.

Corn

Corn is one of America's favorite vegetables. We like to eat it on the cob. We grind it into meal and make corn bread. We sometimes grind it into a fine powder which we use to put on little babies' bodies after they are bathed. Corn is even used sometimes in making soap.

When Christopher Columbus found his way to our part of the world in 1492, he had never seen corn. He was served corn by the Native Americans. The Native Americans called corn "maize." When Columbus sailed back home, he took corn kernels with him. Soon the people of Spain had a new vegetable to enjoy.

Corn is easy to grow. For that reason, many home gardeners plant it. You, too, can grow it. All you need is a little sunny land, plenty of water, and some fertilizer.

Dig up the area that gets sun all day. Be sure to get the soil very loose, get the rocks out, and break up any clumps of dirt. Form the soil into hills or mounds. In the top of each mound put one or two kernels of corn. Bury it about three inches deep. Keep the soil damp until the kernel begins to sprout. In a few days you will see a little green stem called a stalk. After this your corn will grow fast. It will be six feet tall. On each stalk there will be several ears of corn. At the end of each ear are strings called "silk." When the silk turns brown, the corn is ready to pick and eat.

DITTO #100, WRITING YOUR OWN TEST QUESTIONS

Directions: Write five questions to go with this selection. Use another sheet of paper.

Animal Homes

Animal homes can be found almost anywhere—up in trees, on the ground, and under the ground. There are animals in the coldest climates and in the hottest lands.

When you think of tree dwellers, you probably see a bird's nest in your mind's eye, but there are other animals that build nests in trees—the squirrel, for example. Birds' nests are made of string, leaves and twigs while squirrels' nests are usually made only of leaves. Squirrels' nests are somewhat larger. Also living in trees are all kinds of bugs—on leaves you find caterpillars; under the bark you may find grub worms which make wonderful fishing bait. The leaf insect is hard to see because it is the same shape and color as the leaf it sits upon. The walking stick insect looks just like a twig.

Many animals live on the ground in different kinds of houses. The beaver builds its lodge in a river by making a dam of wood and leaves. People build their homes on the ground. Ducks settle down in nests in the tall grass near a pond.

Underground, we find some truly interesting animals. Living in burrows we find ants, rabbits, and moles. Most of these animals stay in their holes all day and forage for food at night.

The next time you are bored, take a paper and pencil and look around your house and yard. You will be surprised by the number of animals that live in the same place you do.

DITTO #101, WRITING YOUR OWN TEST QUESTIONS

Directions: Write five questions to go with this selection. Use another sheet of paper.

Mushrooms

What is a mushroom? Is it meat? Is it a vegetable? Mushrooms are plants. Unlike most plants, however, mushrooms are not green. They are usually white or black. They look like small umbrellas.

Mushrooms are found growing in the woods or are grown on special farms. They grow in places where there is no sunlight or very little sunlight. Instead of plain dirt, they prefer to grow in soil that has lots of dead leaves or rotten wood in it.

For hundreds of years, people have eaten mushrooms. They have gone into the woods to pick them. People who pick mushrooms know how to tell a poisonous mushroom from an "edible" one. Pretty ones and blue mushrooms are always poisonous and will kill if they are eaten.

Mushrooms are best when they are freshly picked. They can be eaten raw or they can be cooked in butter. Raw ones are often put in salads. If you do not plan to use them right away, you can buy canned mushrooms.

DITTO #102, WRITING YOUR OWN TEST QUESTIONS

Directions: Write five questions to go with this selection. Use another sheet of paper.

Sleep

All animals require sleep. Some animals sleep at night while others prefer to sleep during the day. If an animal does not get enough sleep, it will become grouchy or mean. Sleep allows the body to rest. The heart slows down, the breathing slows down, and we relax.

Oddly enough, our brains are often quite active. Many authors say they get ideas for their books while they are asleep. Some keep a paper and pencil by the bed so they can jot down these dream ideas.

Dreams may be good or bad. In dreams we sometimes find an answer to a problem we haven't been able to solve during the day. Sometimes we dream of things we wish would happen. No one likes bad dreams but we all have them. Bad dreams may follow overeating, being sick, or watching a scary or shocking TV show.

Animals' sleep requirements are different. Cats and dogs sleep very lightly, being alert to danger. Bears and snakes hibernate (sleep) all winter without waking for food or when touched. Humans' sleep varies from dozing where every little noise wakes us to very heavy sleep. Most grownups need around eight hours of sleep each day to feel well and many children may need more than that.

THE FIVE ELEMENTS OF A GOOD SENTENCE/PARTS OF SPEECH

You can teach almost anything to anybody provided you come up with a novel way to do it. A novel way to teach children to recognize nouns and verbs (information that is critical to writing a proper sentence) is described in this section. The lessons provided will also help students establish the habit of capitalizing the first word of a sentence and correctly punctuating it.

As soon as a student attains a reading level of about 2.0, you can teach the concepts of nouns, verbs, and phrases. This unit requires about 18 to 20 consecutive days to complete. You will not want to begin the unit unless you can proceed through the unit without missing a day. It is best to begin the unit on Tuesday and allow about an hour for each lesson.

Day 1   On the first day you state the goal: Students will learn how to write good sentences. Daily you have them look at their hand and, using their fingers, name each part of a good sentence. (See Ditto #103.) Review this section three times the first day, twice the second, and once each day thereafter.

Next you will introduce the concept of nouns. Get the students' attention by shouting the words, **"It's a bird! It's a plane! It's Superman!"** all the while pointing at imaginary things in the air. (I guarantee you will have all eyes on you.)

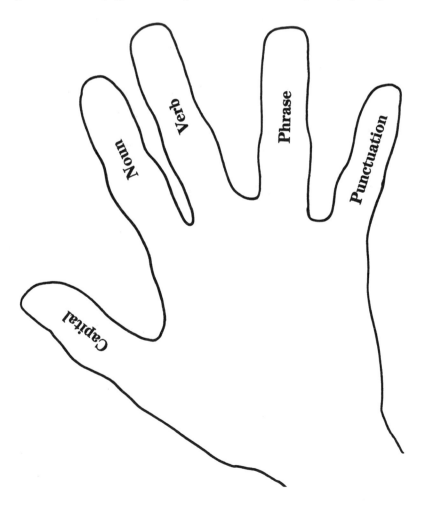

DITTO #103, STUDENT NOTEBOOK HANDOUT,
FIVE ELEMENTS OF A GOOD SENTENCE

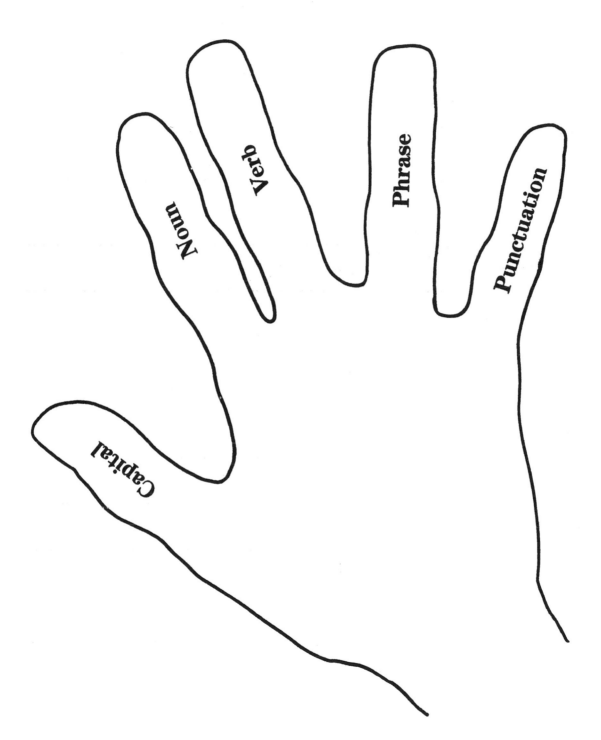

Tell them, "We are going to play a game. At the end of the game, you will be able to recognize words that are nouns. Nouns are usually things we can see or draw." Write on the board and say, "Nouns are the names of people, places, or things." Begin the game by saying, "It's a ..." Going around the room, ask students to rapidly name a noun. If a student cannot think of one, give help by pointing to an object or give a clue (draw a simple picture of a fish) or give a word clue such as "We see them on the table." Students think this is fun, and they like the rapid-fire nature of their responses, so don't let it lag. After each person has a chance to orally participate, you can put some of the nouns they named on the board and have them complete Ditto #104. Circulate to see that the words they put on that ditto are all nouns.

Day 2   Quickly review what you did the first day: "Today you will learn to recognize the helping verbs." By reviewing this information daily and offering the promise of an edible reward for mastery, your students will memorize most—if not all—the helping verbs in about 14 days. Have students look at Ditto #105. Chorally, have them name each verb. It is essential that each child follow along the list with a finger. After four days of group review, have them work in pairs daily for the first few minutes of the period. One partner reads all the words on the list while the other listens. Then the one who read will try to say them from memory to his or her partner. Tell the students that when they can name the entire list with fewer than four omissions, they will get their name on the board, a good note sent home and either a cookie, some peanuts, a candy or some other special privilege. They may do this in front of the class or privately with you or the aide.

You will want to point out to students that the helping verbs have been listed alphabetically to help them remember them.

Day 3   On day 3, review what a noun is, have students name a few, and go over Ditto #105 again. "Today we will learn what a verb is." Say, "A verb is a word that tells what a person is doing. It describes action." On butcher paper make a list of verbs they contribute. Hang these lists around the room.

Day 4   Review quickly what the students have learned during the first three days by having them repeat the definition of a noun, giving a few examples, and naming the helping verbs as well as a few action verbs. Write the following words on the board and ask the students to chorally read it: "A sentence is a complete thought that makes sense." Using Ditto #106, read the first sentence fragment aloud to show it doesn't make sense (until the students complete it). Go over the ditto as a group orally to obtain several ideas for each fragment. At the end of the session, students will complete the ditto by adding a phrase to the sentence so it makes sense.

Days 5 to 20

Review:
1. The five elements of a good sentence (Use Ditto #103 to facilitate memory).
2. The definition of a noun; cite a few examples each day (Ditto #104).
3. Helping verbs (have students list them) (Ditto #105).
4. The definition of a verb; cite a few examples (Ditto #105).
5. The parts of a sentence: *Subject* (noun) *Verb* (helping/action/both) *Phrase*

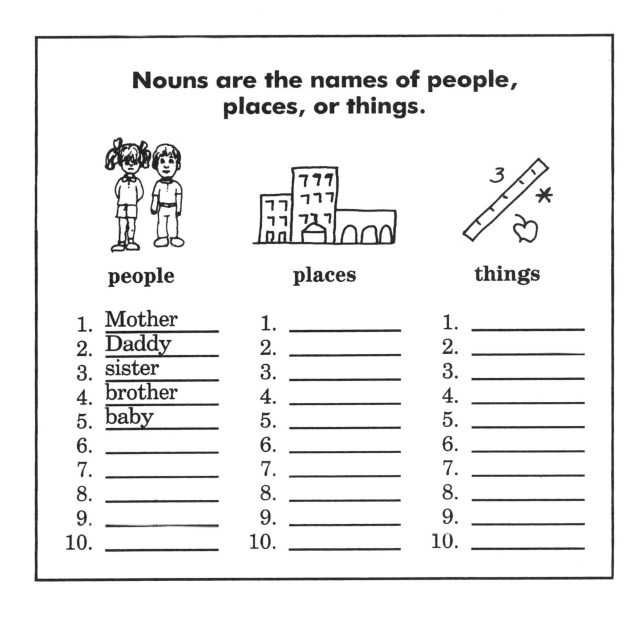

Nouns are the names of people, places, or things.

people

places

things

1. Mother
2. Daddy
3. sister
4. brother
5. baby
6. _____
7. _____
8. _____
9. _____
10. _____

1. _____
2. _____
3. _____
4. _____
5. _____
6. _____
7. _____
8. _____
9. _____
10. _____

1. _____
2. _____
3. _____
4. _____
5. _____
6. _____
7. _____
8. _____
9. _____
10. _____

verbs

Helping Verbs	Some Doing Verbs
am	eat
are	sleep
be	help
been	wash
being	walk
can/can't	talk
could/couldn't	play
do/don't	work
did/didn't	go
does/doesn't	run
had/hadn't	sit
has/hasn't	fall
have/haven't	write
is/isn't	fold
may	jump
must	cut
might	draw
should/shouldn't	print
was/wasn't	underline
were/weren't	read
will/won't	circle
would/wouldn't	and many more

Name _____

DITTO #106, FIVE ELEMENTS OF A GOOD SENTENCE (PHRASES)

Directions: These sentence fragments need a phrase added so that they make sense.

1. I am _____

_____

2. She could see _____

_____

3. Mother doesn't like to _____

_____

4. My Dad went _____

_____

5. We can go to _____

_____

6. The dog was _____

_____

7. Mother told me I had _____

_____

8. The teacher wants us to _____

_____

6. The requirement that the sentence must make sense.

7. Daily sentence-writing practice. Each day students do an envelope not done before. You will need to set up a system so you can record which envelopes each person has done.

Preparing Materials for Sentence Building

Follow the directions on Dittoes #107 through 121. A parent volunteer can usually be enlisted to cut out and mark the materials. (This is not something students can do accurately.) Put the number of the activity on the front of each envelope. This way, if a piece is dropped on the floor, you can get it back into the correct envelope. You may want to put a series of lines on each envelope so students can sign their names when they use that packet.

Procedure for Sentence-Building Activity

First, you will find that for the first four days you do this activity, you need to enlist the help of at least two other adults. After four days, you need one helper. (Parents who read can help. The Rsp might also help you.)

Say, **"I'm going to give you an envelope. Write your name on one of the lines on the front of the envelope. Do not open the envelope until I tell you to."** (Circulate to be sure students put their names on the envelope).

On the board, write the words:

subjects (nouns)   verbs (helping/action)   phrases

Say, **"Do not open the envelope yet. Inside your envelope are slips of paper. Take out one slip."** (Wait for them to comply.) **"Look on the back of the slip. If it says noun, put it on the left side of your desk."** (Demonstrate by taping a card under the word "noun" on the board.) **"If it says verb, place it in the center of your desk. If it says phrase, place it on the right side of your desk."** (Wait.) **"Take out the next slip and place it where it goes."** Have students continue to do this until all the words are out and categorized.

Say, **"Now pull down your nouns. Add a verb and a phrase to the first noun so that you have a sentence that makes sense."** (You and the helpers will circulate and give help until each student has formed one sensible sentence.) **"Look at the next noun and add a verb and phrase to it."** (Again circulate and give help.) Continue this procedure until each student has made four sentences that you have checked to be sure they make sense. At this point, give the students a sheet of paper and ask them to copy their sentences. Remind them they will need to capitalize and punctuate each sentence.

Circulate as students are copying. Have them read a sentence to you. Then if it is copied correctly, put a "smile" sticker by it. As students begin to finish, tell them to put their name on the board. This serves two purposes: (1) you can call students to bring their paper to you, read every sentence to you, and make corrections so you can put a good grade on it; and (2) helpers can go to students whose names are not on the board.

DITTO #107, SENTENCE BUILDING—SET 1

Directions for Teacher: Cut out the nouns and on the back of each piece write <u>Noun 1</u>. Cut out the verbs and on the back label each piece <u>Verb 1</u>. Cut out the phrases and mark each piece as <u>Phrase 1</u>. Place all the pieces in an envelope labeled <u>Sentence Building, Set 1</u>.

Nouns

it	they	my sister
we	I	mother

Verbs

was	ate	did	went
played	is		washed

Phrases

too hot to play outside	
the car	for my dad
a snack	to a movie
in the kitchen	a game
when I got home	my homework
last night	very carefully

DITTO #108, SENTENCE BUILDING—SET 2

Directions for Teacher: Cut out the nouns and on the back of each piece write <u>Noun 2</u>. Cut out the verbs and on the back label each piece <u>Verb 2</u>. Cut out the phrases and mark each piece as <u>Phrase 2</u>. Place all the pieces in an envelope labeled <u>Sentence Building, Set 2</u>.

a white kitten	**I**	**she**
father	**the boy**	**Sam**

Nouns

ran	**wanted**	**went**
ate	**sat**	**had**	**picked**

Verbs

up a tree	**from a tree**
an apple	**on the porch**
to work early today	
a very bad cold	**too much**
to be on the team	
to his friend's house	

Phrases

DITTO #109, SENTENCE BUILDING—SET 3

Directions for Teacher: Cut out the nouns and on the back of each piece write <u>Noun 3</u>. Cut out the verbs and on the back label each piece <u>Verb 3</u>. Cut out the phrases and mark each piece as <u>Phrase 3</u>. Place all the pieces in an envelope labeled <u>Sentence Building, Set 3</u>.

Nouns

we	the teacher	he
she	the neighbor	I

Verbs

are	going	got	had	love
went		wrote		planted

Phrases

from her dad	to the zoo	
on the blackboard		the trees
near the house		a letter
on a trip	this summer	
small pups	a sun tan	

DITTO #110, SENTENCE BUILDING—SET 4

Directions for Teacher: Cut out the nouns and on the back of each piece write <u>Noun 4</u>. Cut out the verbs and on the back label each piece <u>Verb 4</u>. Cut out the phrases and mark each piece as <u>Phrase 4</u>. Place all the pieces in an envelope labeled <u>Sentence Building, Set 4</u>.

the cookies	mom	she	I

the two sisters	my brother

Nouns

is	are	did	was

read	going	look

put	went	swimming

Verbs

a very good snack	to bed

just alike	on the table

my homework	last night

in the lake	a poem

Phrases

DITTO #111, SENTENCE BUILDING—SET 5

Directions for Teacher: Cut out the nouns and on the back of each piece write <u>Noun 5</u>. Cut out the verbs and on the back label each piece <u>Verb 5</u>. Cut out the phrases and mark each piece as <u>Phrase 5</u>. Place all the pieces in an envelope labeled <u>Sentence Building, Set 5</u>.

the postman	the cat	he	**Nouns**
mother	a boy	they	

was	playing	were	left	**Verbs**
eating	lives	running		
made	did not go	is		

after the mouse	five letters	**Phrases**
a big batch of cookies	with us	
with the dog	on a trip	
next door	very cute	

DITTO #112, SENTENCE BUILDING—SET 6

Directions for Teacher: Cut out the nouns and on the back of each piece write <u>Noun 6</u>. Cut out the verbs and on the back label each piece <u>Verb 6</u>. Cut out the phrases and mark each piece as <u>Phrase 6</u>. Place all the pieces in an envelope labeled <u>Sentence Building, Set 6</u>.

Nouns

the girl	we	my parents
Nicole	the plane	she

Verbs

was	feeding	studied	is
played	are	washing	swam
crashed	having		playing

Phrases

late last night		a race
in the backyard		a game
in a field	her dog	the car
across the pool		with us

DITTO #113, SENTENCE BUILDING—SET 7

Directions for Teacher: Cut out the nouns and on the back of each piece write <u>Noun 7</u>. Cut out the verbs and on the back label each piece <u>Verb 7</u>. Cut out the phrases and mark each piece as <u>Phrase 7</u>. Place all the pieces in an envelope labeled <u>Sentence Building, Set 7</u>.

Nouns

my father	they	she
the cat	I	the child

Verbs

are	is	did	found
can	climb		eating
was	playing		win

Phrases

all their homework		
the race	a game	very cold
his dinner		that tree
a nice rock		about 5 years old

DITTO #114, SENTENCE BUILDING—SET 8

Directions for Teacher: Cut out the nouns and on the back of each piece write <u>Noun 8</u>. Cut out the verbs and on the back label each piece <u>Verb 8</u>. Cut out the phrases and mark each piece as <u>Phrase 8</u>. Place all the pieces in an envelope labeled <u>Sentence Building, Set 8</u>.

Nouns

wildflowers		my brother	
we	you	cows	my dad

Verbs

bloomed		loves		works
had	did	grazed		sat
walked		remembered		

Phrases

to read	on the side of the hill
very hard	at the post office
in the shade of the big oak tree	
my birthday	all over the meadow

DITTO #115, SENTENCE BUILDING—SET 9

Directions for Teacher: Cut out the nouns and on the back of each piece write <u>Noun 9</u>. Cut out the verbs and on the back label each piece <u>Verb 9</u>. Cut out the phrases and mark each piece as <u>Phrase 9</u>. Place all the pieces in an envelope labeled <u>Sentence Building, Set 9</u>.

mother	we	father
I	he	she

Nouns

went	can	go	had
will	likes		make
found	read		saw

Verbs

when I get home	for you
to the store	a little puppy
the newspaper	his bike
to a movie	a cake	to school

Phrases

DITTO #116, SENTENCE BUILDING—SET 10

Directions for Teacher: Cut out the nouns and on the back of each piece write <u>Noun 10</u>. Cut out the verbs and on the back label each piece <u>Verb 10</u>. Cut out the phrases and mark each piece as <u>Phrase 10</u>. Place all the pieces in an envelope labeled <u>Sentence Building, Set 10</u>.

Nouns

mom	that bird	I
we	my dad	they

Verbs

made	ate	flew	will
can	climb		cut down
gave	draw		ride

Phrases

the cake	for me	a worm
over the fence		my bike
a picture	that tree	a gift
to the bride and groom		

DITTO #117, SENTENCE BUILDING—SET 11

Directions for Teacher: Cut out the nouns and on the back of each piece write <u>Noun 11</u>. Cut out the verbs and on the back label each piece <u>Verb 11</u>. Cut out the phrases and mark each piece as <u>Phrase 11</u>. Place all the pieces in an envelope labeled <u>Sentence Building, Set 11</u>.

mother	daddy	we	**Nouns**
Sally	I	she	

cooked		worked	has got	**Verbs**
have	grew	took	swam	

very hard	most of our meals	**Phrases**
at the pool	some vegetables	
a model train	swimming lessons	
a letter	from my uncle	

DITTO #118, SENTENCE BUILDING—SET 12

Directions for Teacher: Cut out the nouns and on the back of each piece write <u>Noun 12</u>. Cut out the verbs and on the back label each piece <u>Verb 12</u>. Cut out the phrases and mark each piece as <u>Phrase 12</u>. Place all the pieces in an envelope labeled <u>Sentence Building, Set 12</u>.

Nouns

the old man	he	the boy
the girl	mother	father

Verbs

will	cook	went	was
reading	fell	can	make
found		is		playing

Phrases

if he has to	to the store
for some flour	a book
out of a tree	her own clothes
some money	in the sand
on the sidewalk	a game

DITTO #119, SENTENCE BUILDING—SET 13

Directions for Teacher: Cut out the nouns and on the back of each piece write <u>Noun 13</u>. Cut out the verbs and on the back label each piece <u>Verb 13</u>. Cut out the phrases and mark each piece as <u>Phrase 13</u>. Place all the pieces in an envelope labeled <u>Sentence Building, Set 13</u>.

she	the store	the paper	**Nouns**
the baby	he	the teacher	

sat		will be	crying	**Verbs**
is	was	reading	like	
would	make	slept	open	

under a tree	on my desk	**Phrases**
all night long	the picture	
all by himself	at 7:00 A.M.	
to help	a story	

DITTO #120, SENTENCE BUILDING—SET 14

Directions for Teacher: Cut out the nouns and on the back of each piece write <u>Noun 14</u>. Cut out the verbs and on the back label each piece <u>Verb 14</u>. Cut out the phrases and mark each piece as <u>Phrase 14</u>. Place all the pieces in an envelope labeled <u>Sentence Building, Set 14</u>.

Nouns

the bird	the ball	the teacher
my dog	the car	she

Verbs

flew	rolled	ran	didn't
taught		crashed	find

Phrases

over the fence	the lesson
into the street	into the tree
after the cat	her lost coat
us a new song	

DITTO #121, SENTENCE BUILDING—SET 15

Directions for Teacher: Cut out the nouns and on the back of each piece write <u>Noun 15</u>. Cut out the verbs and on the back label each piece <u>Verb 15</u>. Cut out the phrases and mark each piece as <u>Phrase 15</u>. Place all the pieces in an envelope labeled <u>Sentence Building, Set 15</u>.

			Nouns
my brother	father	the doctor	
my sister	my uncle	the baby	

				Verbs
went	sat	talked	sleeping	
was	is	washed	came	
likes	walked	played		

			Phrases
to work	in the yard	the car	
to visit	to her friend		
for two hours	on the couch		
in her crib	to our house		

ALPHABETIZING BY FIRST AND SECOND LETTERS

This is a skill you will need to teach before students will be able to look up words in a dictionary. You may want to determine students can alphabetize by first letter before you start teaching this more complicated skill.

In this section, you will find only two dittoes #122-123 to use for your guided practice sessions. Using the "500 Most Used Words List" you can construct other dittoes so students can continue to practice independently until they are proficient at this skill.

WRITING STORIES REVISITED

Before you give students dittoes #124 through 128, you will want to remind them that stories have a beginning, middle, and end. You may also want to do some brainstorming as a group. For example, Ditto #124 concerns camping. You may want to precede its use by having a discussion where children share orally their camping experiences. If the discussion is sparse, you can add a story or two from your imagination or experience. This will help the child who has never camped out to have something to write about. Likewise, some children may not have ever visited grandma. A discussion of the kinds of things children do at their grandparents' houses may help the child without that experience to be able to "make up" a story.

Name _____

DITTO #122, ALPHABETIZING BY FIRST AND SECOND LETTERS

Directions:
- Circle the first letter of each word.
- Alphabetize words by the first letter.
- Look at the second letter of the words that have the same beginning letter.
- List the words in order using the second letter to help.

1. bed   b_____

2. grow   b_____

3. wet   g_____

4. keep   k_____

5. bugs   l _____

6. seeds   p_____

7. live   s _____

8. soil   s _____

9. water   w _____

10. plant   w _____

Name _____

DITTO #123, ALPHABETIZING BY FIRST AND SECOND LETTERS

Directions:
- Circle the first letter of each word.
- Alphabetize words by the first letter.
- Look at the second letter of the words that have the same beginning letter.
- List the words in order using the second letter to help.

1. could _____

2. and _____

3. came _____

4. eat _____

5. have _____

6. many _____

7. ask _____

8. just _____

9. home _____

10. much _____

DITTO #124, WRITING STORIES (REVISITED)

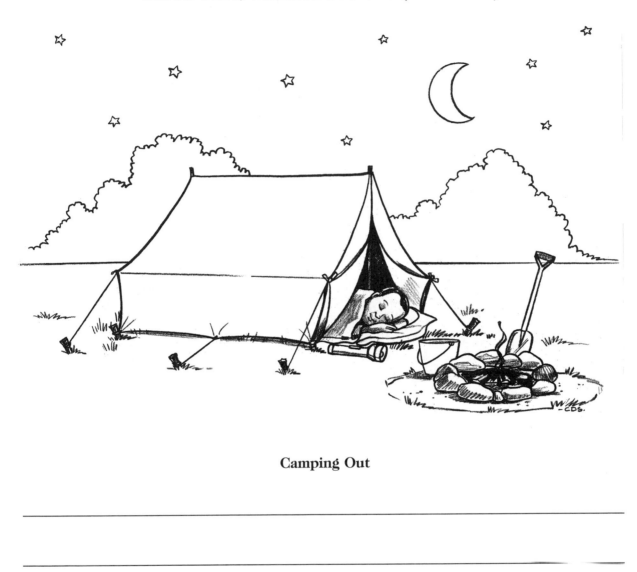

Camping Out

_____

_____

_____

_____

_____

_____

_____

Name _____

DITTO #125, WRITING STORIES (REVISITED)

A Visit with Grandma

© 1995 by The Center for Applied Research in Education

_____

_____

_____

_____

_____

_____

_____

DITTO #126, WRITING STORIES (REVISITED)

Spending the Night

_____

_____

_____

_____

_____

_____

_____

DITTO #127, WRITING STORIES (REVISITED)

Directions: Write a story about going to a zoo. Be sure to have a beginning, middle, and end.

Going to the Zoo

_____

_____

_____

_____

_____

_____

DITTO #128, WRITING STORIES (REVISITED)

Directions: Write a story about an old house that looks haunted. Be sure to have a beginning, middle, and end.

The Haunted House

_____

_____

_____

_____

_____

_____

_____

MATERIALS
FOR STUDENTS FUNCTIONING
AT LEVEL 3.0 TO 4.0

Objectives for Level 3.0 to 4.0

- Given five paragraphs to read, _____ will read them and correctly find the main idea in four out of the five (80% accuracy).

- Given 20 words, _____ will match them with their synonyms with 100% accuracy.

- Given two lists of five sentences each, _____ will be able to accurately determine whether the correct punctuation is a period or a question mark (100% accuracy).

- Given ten questions and an index, _____ will locate the key word, use the index, and find the correct page number for the information with 80% accuracy in a 50-minute period (writes page number).

- Given ten singular nouns, _____ will apply the rules and write the plural form with 100% accuracy.

- Given a topic sentence (or main idea), _____ will write a paragraph of at least three sentences, correcting all errors under supervision, three times a week for four months.

- Given an outline, _____ will write a two- to five-paragraph report, correcting all errors under supervision, two times a week for four months.

- After writing a report, _____ will stand before the class or before a small group and tell what he or she learned from doing the report, once a week for four months.

The balance of this book is devoted to materials specifically to meet the needs of older students who are either LD, low achievers, or at risk. The materials in Unit 5 are written at a functional level of 3.0 to 4.0, and students using them may be in junior high or even senior high school. (See the Cumulative Deficit Chart in Chapter 7 of Volume I.)

Upper-Grade Reading Passages and Suggestions for Using Them

In Chapter 11 of Volume I, we talked about different methods for teaching reading. The passages given here on Dittoes #129 through 135 can be used with the cloze technique. They may also be used as alternative assignments for American History.

If you want to use them for a cloze activity, make a reproduced copy and white-out the words in the underlined spaces. Then number each space. Students write their best guess for what would make sense in the space on a separate answer sheet. In correcting a cloze activity, accept any answer that makes sense. It is also important to tell students that they are not expected to make 100%. If they get 50% to 75% of the words correct, that is average performance; 75% and up is excellent performance. What you hope to see is that a student will improve in performance as he or she has more experiences with cloze.

A third way to use these selections is to have students write study questions for them.

Name _____

DITTO 129, UPPER-GRADE READING PASSAGE

Directions: Listen to the directions your teacher will give.

The Mayflower, the Pilgrims, and Plymouth Village

Every November, we celebrate Thanksgiving. You hear something <u>about</u> the Mayflower, the Pilgrims, <u>and</u> the Indians.

The word "pilgrim" <u>is</u> a word that refers <u>to</u> a person who goes wandering, looking <u>for</u> something. The Pilgrims who boarded the Mayflower <u>in</u> 1620 had many reasons for wandering. At that time in England, the King of England had declared <u>that</u> the official church for England was his church, which meant that if <u>you</u> did not believe in the <u>same</u> things as the King, your life would <u>be</u> made uncomfortable. The <u>people</u> who did not see things the <u>way</u> the King did wanted to worship in their own fashion so they wanted to leave. A second <u>group</u> of people were the poor. At that time in England if you stole a loaf <u>of</u> bread or could <u>not</u> pay your bills, you <u>went</u> to jail. These people <u>hoped</u> to have better lives in the new land.

The Mayflower sailed <u>with</u> 102 people on board. After 65 uncomfortable days, <u>it</u> arrived in what is now Massachusetts at a place <u>called</u> Plymouth Rock on December 26. Winter descended before the Pilgrims had time to get <u>ready</u> for it. Half the settlers died.

In the spring, friendly Indians taught the <u>Pilgrims</u> to plant corn and other crops. When it was time to harvest the <u>food</u>, the Pilgrims felt it was appropriate to <u>invite</u> the Indians who had helped them to their feast of thanks.

Name _____

DITTO #130, UPPER-GRADE READING PASSAGE

Directions: Listen to the directions your teacher gives you.

Life in the Colonies

What was it like to live in colonial <u>times</u>? Since there were no electric lights, <u>people</u> tended to go to bed early <u>and</u> get up early. Days were busy. Large families <u>were</u> typical. Sometimes the grandparents lived <u>in</u> the home. Everyone in the <u>family</u> over six years old worked.

Boys helped their fathers, while girls helped their <u>mothers</u>. Most children were taught <u>to</u> read and do simple math. Some were <u>taught</u> at home; some went to a "Dame's house" (a widow who tutored <u>children</u>); a few went to school (usually those children with wealthy parents). For all but the children of the "betters," it was a custom <u>for</u> a boy child to be apprenticed to a craftsman <u>from</u> about age 7 to age 18. While working and living with the craftsman, the <u>child</u> gradually learned the trade—making furniture, <u>making</u> items from glass, silver, leather, or making candles. Girls <u>learned</u> to spin, make cloth, sew, <u>and cook</u>. If the child <u>lived</u> in the middle colonies or the southern colonies, farming <u>was</u> the way of life.

People often worked six days a <u>week</u> but not on the Sabbath (Sunday). In New England, Sunday was church day and church services often lasted several hours. After <u>church</u>, children played while parents visited with friends.

All in <u>all</u>, life was pretty good. If a person <u>worked</u> hard, the result was a <u>better</u> standard of living.

Name _____

DITTO #131, UPPER GRADE READING PASSAGE

Directions: Listen to the directions your teacher will give.

The Approach of the American Revolutionary War

The colonies in our country grew rapidly. Within 12 years after the Plymouth colony <u>was</u> established there were 20,000 Englishmen living <u>in</u> the area they called New England. In a matter of a few years, <u>there</u> were thirteen colonies—running from Massachusetts down <u>the</u> eastern coast all the way <u>to</u> Georgia.

The colonists made things to sell in England and the English <u>made</u> things to sell in the colonies and all was well until <u>the</u> King decided that the colonists needed to pay more taxes. After all, he <u>had</u> provided them with soldiers to <u>fight</u> their war against the French and Indians and had had to keep <u>troops</u> in the colonies ever since. The colonists didn't see it <u>that</u> way and the trouble <u>began</u>. The King decided all goods traveling between the two lands would <u>have</u> to travel in English (British) ships. This angered the <u>colonists</u>.

One blunder followed another. Next, the King put taxes <u>on</u> sugar. The colonists stopped buying <u>sugar</u>. Then the King put a tax on all newspapers and legal documents. The colonists reacted <u>by</u> beating up the tax collectors. The cry went up, "Taxation without representation is tyranny!" But the King paid <u>no</u> attention because he considered it his right to <u>tax</u> his subjects as he pleased and they had no say in the matter. It is not surprising that a movement that suggested the colonies separate from England and form their <u>own</u> country began. The King began to send more troops to New England to control any situation that <u>arose</u>. At that time, it was necessary for many of these soldiers to be quartered in private homes.

When the King taxed tea, a group called "the Sons of Liberty" disguised themselves <u>as</u> Indians and threw the <u>tea</u> into Boston Harbor in an incident now known as "The Boston Tea Party."

To punish the colonists, the King decided to close Boston Harbor <u>and</u> block the roads into the city, so food didn't come in. Mobs threw rocks at soldiers. Soldiers retaliated toward the colonists and killed a few.

In 1775, Patrick Henry, a colonist, <u>gave</u> a fiery speech ending in the words "Give me Liberty or give me death!" He vocalized aloud what other <u>men</u> such as John Adams and Benjamin Franklin were saying to smaller groups.

War became inevitable. The leaders of the revolution sought out General George Washington to head the colonists' army. Weapons <u>were</u> made in homes. Wives allowed their silver utensils to be turned <u>into</u> the shells for ammunition. Groups of young men who called themselves "the minutemen" rode out into the countryside to <u>train</u> for battle.

The war began on April 19, 1775 at Lexington, Massachusetts, when a group of the town's men confronted a <u>group</u> of soldiers on the Lexington Green. The town's women watched their husbands die from the windows of their <u>homes</u>. When colonists and British soldiers met on Concord Bridge, someone fired "the shot heard round the world." The War was on! It <u>lasted</u> for eight long years.

Name _____

DITTO #132, UPPER-GRADE READING PASSAGE

Directions: Listen to the directions your teacher will give.

Establishing a Government for the New Country

The First Continental Congress met in Philadelphia <u>in</u> September, 1774. The representatives of the colonists knew <u>they</u> must deal with the King <u>of</u> England and defend their rights. It <u>was</u> decided there would be no trade with Britain unless the abuses stopped.

The abuses increased <u>and</u> war broke out in April of 1775.

The Second Continental Congress <u>met</u> in July of 1776. The leaders signed <u>the</u> Declaration of Independence which was written <u>by</u> Thomas Jefferson. The colonies declared themselves free from British rule.

The government was weak. It was without authority. There were <u>many</u> problems to be taken care <u>of</u>. In 1787, 55 men <u>from</u> 12 colonies met in Philadelphia <u>to</u> define what functions the federal government would <u>have</u> and what powers the states would retain. The Constitution was written.

The first ten amendments <u>are</u> called "the Bill of Rights" and they address and guarantee the <u>rights</u> of the individual citizen. The individual has:

- Freedom of speech, religion, the press, and peaceable assembly.

- The right to keep and bear arms.

- Freedom from having to quarter soldiers in their homes.

- The right to privacy in their houses, persons, papers and effects; to be free from searches and seizures unless a court orders it based on sound evidence that there is a good <u>reason</u> to do it.

- The right to a trial by a jury of peers; the right not to say <u>anything</u> that will incriminate him- or herself; the right to be compensated for his or her property if it is taken by the government.

- The right to a speedy trial, to confront his or her accused, bail, and freedom from cruel or unusual punishments.

All of the rights outlined above were <u>rights</u> that the representatives felt King George <u>had</u> violated. It is not surprising, therefore, that the colonists <u>decided</u> they did not want a <u>king</u> as a leader. It was decided there would be an elected government—president and vice president—who had limited powers unlike the King; and two houses of Congress who <u>would</u> make the laws. It established a court system that would judge whether those laws were made under the guidelines set by the Constitution and would hear cases of individuals, being very careful to ensure the person's constitutional rights were <u>not</u> violated.

The constitution had 12 Amendments in 1804. It allowed for the addition of <u>others</u> as a need developed for them. Today, <u>there</u> are 26 Amendments.

There were many famous patriots but the <u>one</u> most loved and respected was George Washington, who led the Continental Armies to victory (1783) in the Revolutionary War and was elected as the new <u>country's</u> first president at the Constitutional Convention of 1787.

Name _____

DITTO #133, UPPER-GRADE READING PASSAGE

Directions: Listen to the directions your teacher gives you.

Go West, Young Man!

England was not the only country that sent <u>settlers</u> to the new world. French explorers <u>and</u> Spanish explorers came earlier <u>than</u> the English.

The French <u>hoped</u> to find gold and silver but did not. They did <u>find</u> a rich supply of fur-bearing animals living <u>in</u> the woods near <u>the</u> Ohio and Mississippi rivers. Settlements grew up along these <u>rivers</u>. The territory occupied by the French ran from the Gulf coast all the <u>way</u> north into Canada. The area <u>was</u> called Louisiana and was named for King Louis <u>of</u> France.

The Spanish were also establishing settlements in the <u>new</u> world at the same <u>time</u> as the French and English. <u>They</u> settled in Florida, the area of El Paso, Texas and Santa Fe, New Mexico. They also moved into what <u>is</u> now California, establishing large farms called "Ranchos" and building Catholic Missions.

The population of the young nation <u>grew</u> steadily. Large families were the rule and many more <u>people</u> streamed to the new land in hopes of bettering <u>their</u> lives. Many were poor and were enticed <u>by</u> the stories of free land. When New England was full and <u>there</u> was no more open land, they were <u>instructed</u> to "go west," so they <u>did</u>.

The Indians <u>who</u> had been friendly and helpful <u>to</u> the early settlers were becoming hostile. The white <u>man</u> had pushed them off their <u>lands</u> and disregarded their rights.

Name _____

DITTO #134, UPPER-GRADE READING PASSAGE

Directions: Listen to the directions your teacher gives.

Growth and Change

The years between 1800 and 1860 were a period <u>of</u> growth for the young country. The population increased rapidly. At the time of <u>the</u> Revolutionary War, there <u>were</u> about 2 million people <u>in</u> the United States. This number <u>rose</u> to about 20 million in just 30 years <u>and</u> kept rising steadily as more and <u>more</u> immigrants arrived <u>from</u> Europe.

From the original 13 colonies lining the east <u>coast</u> in 1776, the United <u>States</u> in 1860 had 34 states and its land <u>ran</u> from coast to coast. The country acquired new land in <u>two</u> ways—it bought <u>land</u>, such as the Louisiana Purchase in 1803, and it <u>took</u> land from Mexico in battles.

In 1776, people <u>made</u> their living farming <u>or</u> by working in small shops. During the early 1800s, the U.S. economy expanded rapidly. Factories sprang <u>up</u>. New machinery made it <u>possible</u> to mass-produce items formerly <u>made</u> by hand. The steamboat and the train were <u>invented</u>, making it possible to <u>move</u> large amounts of goods from place to <u>place</u>. At that time children often <u>labored</u> in factories for 10 to 12 <u>hours</u> a day. There were public schools but only a few children could attend.

In 1848 gold was discovered in California. <u>When</u> news reached the east coast, thousands of men left <u>home</u> to go to California in <u>hopes</u> of becoming rich.

Name _____

DITTO #135, UPPER-GRADE READING PASSAGE

Directions: Listen to the directions your teacher gives.

The Pony Express

Pushing their horses to the limit, daring horseback riders <u>rode</u> at top speed! Every 10 <u>to</u> 15 miles, they came to <u>a</u> station. There, the station master stood waiting <u>for</u> them with a fresh horse. In a flash, the Pony <u>Express</u> rider transferred the mail sacks to the new <u>horse</u> and took off again. The <u>year</u> was 1860. Daily, for the <u>next</u> 18 months, the brave young <u>riders</u> of the Pony Express carried the <u>mail</u> across country in record time.

The men <u>who</u> started the Pony Express wanted to <u>prove</u> they could deliver mail <u>faster</u> than the stagecoaches. There <u>were</u> no paved roads. It often <u>took</u> a stagecoach 22 days to travel <u>across</u> country. The Pony Express riders <u>did</u> it in 10 days.

It was dangerous <u>work</u> because riders single-handedly had to defend <u>themselves</u> against Indians and bandits. Only once <u>in</u> the history of the Pony Express was the <u>mail</u> ever lost.

The young <u>men</u> were well paid for their 250-mile-a-day runs. To cover the costs, the <u>price</u> of delivering a letter was $5.00. Today the post office <u>delivers</u> that same-sized letter for 32¢ to 55¢ in <u>about</u> 3 to 5 days. The slogan of the post <u>office</u> is "neither snow nor rain nor heat <u>nor</u> gloom of night stays these couriers from the swift completion of their appointed rounds"; but no modern-day postman ever faces the hardships the young men of the Pony Express <u>faced</u>! The Pony Express ended when the telegraph <u>was</u> invented.

DITTO #136, UPPER-GRADE READING PASSAGE

Directions: Listen to the directions your teacher gives.

The Civil War

The 13 original colonies—from Massachusetts southward through Georgia—developed differently. Many of the settlers of the northern colonies had been poor. Some had been "indentured servants." This meant that, in trade for their trip to the new world, the person would send part of his wages for several years to the person who paid for his trip. These persons gradually became free men. By 1850, manufacturing was the primary way of earning a living in the northern colonies.

In the southern colonies farming was the way people earned a living. Farmers wanted cheap labor. They sent ships to Africa to buy slaves. Slaves were paid no wages; they had no rights and masters worked them 14 hours a day. While slaves worked, the plantation owners grew rich. Slaves were regarded as property, not people, so members of the family were sold and taken away, never to see their relatives again.

In the north, the idea of slavery was repugnant. To the south, it was an economic necessity because the plantations could not produce the tobacco, rice and cotton without them.

When Abraham Lincoln was elected president, he promised to abolish slavery. The southern states seceded and formed their own government, the "Confederate States of America." This resulted in a four-year war—the Civil War (1861–1865). The south was destroyed—homes were burned; farms were ruined; slaves were freed.

FINDING THE MAIN IDEA/SUPPORTING DETAILS

When a student reaches a functional level of 3.0, we want to teach him or her how to find the main idea and supporting details in a paragraph. Writing these down becomes a form of note taking. In this section, you will find a series of paragraphs specifically designed to help students gain some confidence in this skill. In these paragraphs, a conscious effort has been made to put the main idea either first or last, and students should be encouraged to do this in their own writing. If the main idea always came first in a paragraph, it would make it possible for us to scan a book's contents extremely quickly; but sometimes we tell our audience the details and then sum them up with the main idea.

As students become proficient at finding the main idea, you can begin to have them look at paragraphs from texts.

For the first few days you may need to do Dittoes #137 through 140 as a guided practice activity. Once students get the hang of it, these can be used for homework or independent practice seatwork. (The paragraphs in the previous section on American History can be used for further practice in locating the main idea once students are fairly proficient at the skill.)

DITTO #137, FINDING THE MAIN IDEA/SUPPORTING DETAILS

Directions: Your job is to first locate and write the main idea (M.I.) of each paragraph. Remember that most authors will put the main idea either first or last in the paragraph. Next, locate the supporting details (S.D.) and write them.

Diamonds are created when carbon is subjected to intense heat and pressure. A flawless diamond will be totally clear. Some diamonds are flawed, which means you can see a tiny black spot of carbon in them.

M.I._____

S.D. _____

S.D. _____

My throat tickles. My nose is running. I feel hot one minute and cold the next. I am getting sick.

M.I._____

S.D. _____

S.D. _____

S.D. _____

Blizzards are heavy snowstorms. The snow fall is so thick that roads are closed. Cattle in the field may freeze to death.

M.I._____

S.D. _____

S.D. _____

DITTO #138, FINDING THE MAIN IDEA/SUPPORTING DETAILS

Directions: Your job is to first locate and write the main idea (M.I.) of each paragraph. Remember that the main idea is often either the first or last sentence in the paragraph. Next, locate the supporting details (S.D.) and write them.

In the middle ages, knights wore armor when going into battle. Armor protected the man from his opponent's blows. A light coat of metal armor called "mail" covered the head, arms, legs, and body.

M.I._____

S.D. _____

S.D. _____

Tarantulas are very large, dark, hairy spiders. They may measure 7 inches across. Their bite usually is not serious.

M.I._____

S.D. _____

S.D. _____

They were strange looking contraptions with huge wooden wheels. They made weird, frightening noises. Some were steam driven, some ran on electricity, and some ran on gasoline. The first automobiles were nothing like the dependable, comfortable vehicles we have today.

M.I._____

S.D. _____

S.D. _____

S.D. _____

Name _____

DITTO #139, FINDING THE MAIN IDEA/SUPPORTING DETAILS

Directions: Your job is to first locate and write the main idea (M.I.) of each paragraph. Remember that the main idea is often either the first or last sentence in the paragraph. Next, locate the supporting details (S.D.) and write them.

Hydrofoils are a different kind of boat. They do not float on top of the water. When the hydrofoil engine is turned on, a cushion of air lifts the boat off the water. Hydrofoil boats are able to move extremely quickly and smoothly.

M.I._____

S.D. _____

S.D. _____

S.D. _____

There are two kinds of dogs—purebred dogs and mutts. The purebred dogs have distinct characteristics. One example of a purebred dog is the Chinese pug with its flat face and bulging eyes. Mutts come in all colors, sizes, and shapes.

M.I._____

S.D. _____

S.D. _____

S.D. _____

Glass is made when sand is heated until it melts. The glassblower picks up a wad of melted glass with a metal tube. As he or she blows through the tube and turns the tube, the glass is shaped into objects of great beauty.

M.I._____

S.D. _____

S.D. _____

Name _____

DITTO #140, FINDING THE MAIN IDEA/SUPPORTING DETAILS

Directions: Your job is to first locate and write the main idea (M.I.) of each paragraph. Remember that the main idea is often either the first or last sentence in the paragraph. Next, locate the supporting details (S.D.) and write them.

Venice, Italy is one of the most unusual cities in the world. The city is composed of many islands. You move from island to island by either walking over the bridges that join the islands or riding in a boat. There are no cars, trucks or motor vehicles allowed in the city.

M.I. _____

S.D. _____

S.D. _____

S.D. _____

"Look! A falling star!" We watched a streak of light cross the heavens. In reality, a falling star is a piece of rock called a meteorite that burns up as it comes through the Earth's atmosphere.

M.I. _____

S.D. _____

Bats prefer dark places. They live in caves, old houses, and deep forests. They rest during the day and fly around looking for food at night.

M.I. _____

S.D. _____

S.D. _____

LEARNING TO USE A DICTIONARY

One of the skills good students need is the ability to use a dictionary efficiently. This is one of the easiest skills to teach but, for some reason, it is rarely taught well. Learning to use the dictionary can be fun. Students enjoy speed and power drills.

It is helpful if you can arrange to have one adult to assist each eight students for the first five days. After that, you can do speed and power drills alone.

On the first day, write the alphabet on the board in a single row:

a b c d e f g h i j k l m n o p q r s t u v w x y z

Show students that the halfway point is approximately m.

Give out the dictionaries and have students hold the dictionary as shown in the illustration. Ask students to try to find the midpoint and open the book. Did it open on l or m?

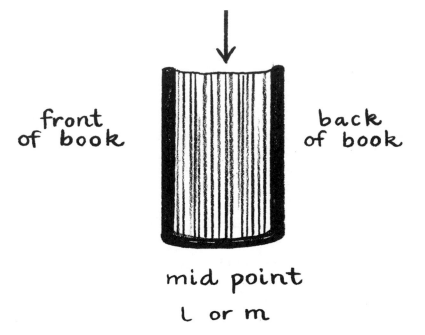

The next thing to show students is the guide words at the top of the page. Show them that the first word on that page appears at the top of the page; the other word is the last word on the page.

Have the students close their dictionaries. Say, **"If the middle of the dictionary is l or m, which way will you go to find a word that begins with c?"** Name some other letters and have the students signal by pointing which way that letter would be from the midpoint of the dictionary.

Have the students hold their dictionaries upright. Tell them you will put a word on the board, for example, eight. Ask them to try to find the e section. Have them signal with a raised hand once they have found any e page. Circulate to see they are all in the e section. Say, **"Good. You found the e section. Let's look to see what the next letter in our word is. It is an i. Look at your guide words. What is the second letter of the words** on the page you are on? Which way will you need to go to find a word that has an i for the second letter?" (Circulate and give help.)

Practice finding words daily, giving help when needed. After about five days most students will have mastered the skill, freeing you to help those who are still having trouble.

You can make this fun by putting everyone's name on the board. Give a word and start timing the students. Record the names and the number of seconds taken for the first five students to locate the word. Do this for several days, after which patterns will arise—some students will consistently be in the first five. At that point, allow those students to be leaders for groups of four less-able students. Then these groups will record who found the word first and who found it second. After several days, everyone will be catching on.

Next, you will want to explain that the dictionary gives a pronunciation key. Let the students look up words from "Words That Drive Kids Crazy" (see Chapter 12 in Volume I) and study the pronunciation key. You need to do this as a group so that less-able students will benefit, too.

When you want to teach vocabulary, use the suggestions in Chapter 12 of Volume I.

DITTO #141, USING A DICTIONARY

Have you ever been to Disneyland or Walt Disney World? Every year millions of people visit one of the amusement parks bearing the famous Disney name. These parks offer attractions for people of all ages.

Young children shout with glee when they meet Mickey Mouse, Goofy, or Snow White and the Seven Dwarfs on the streets of the park. They love to ride the spinning Tea Cups. Older children thrill to the adventure of The Haunted House and the submarine that takes them beneath the water to view rare fish, coral reefs, and even mermaids.

For older people there are wonderful <u>exhibits</u> that show how things were in the past and others that predict how they will be in the future. One such exhibit displays telephones of the future that will allow you to see the person you are calling.

1. What title would you give this selection?

   _____

   _____

2. Using a dictionary, tell what "exhibit" means.

   _____

   _____

3. Do you foresee any kind of problems that might arise from the use of the telephone that lets you see the person you are talking with?_____

   _____

   _____

   _____

   _____

DITTO #142, USING A DICTIONARY

Cacti is a term that refers to a variety of plants found in very dry places such as deserts. A cactus can live and grow in places where there is little rainfall because it is able to store water within itself for later use. Since all cacti are covered with needles, animals leave them alone.

When it does rain, the cactus draws the water into its long roots or into its leaves. During dry periods, it uses its stored water <u>sparingly</u>.

There are many kinds of cacti. Two of the most popular are the barrel cactus and the beaver-tail cactus. The barrel cactus has no leaves. It is a rounded stump; but if the top is cut off and the pulp squeezed, it can yield several quarts of liquid. The beaver-tail cactus has huge rounded leaves that make a delicious vegetable when properly prepared.

1. What title would you give this selection?

   _____

   _____

2. Using your dictionary, and the context of the sentence, what do you think the word "sparingly" means? _____

   _____

   _____

3. The barrel cactus has saved the lives of several people who have been lost on the desert. Can you explain how? _____

   _____

   _____

   _____

Name _____

DITTO #143, USING A DICTIONARY

Have you heard of the Loch Ness monster? The people of Scotland tell stories of a giant sea creature that surfaces out of the depths of Loch Ness—a thirty-mile long, one-mile wide, and very deep body of water in Northern Scotland.

These sightings are rare but persistent. The first occurred around the year 500. During the 1930s, there was an increase in the sightings. In the 1960s, a group of scientists took a small submarine and travelled from one end of the Loch to the other, but to no avail. They said their search did not eliminate the possibility that there might be a few such creatures there. The water in the Loch was filled with peat and, therefore, they could only see a few feet beyond their ship.

If the creatures do <u>exist</u> there, they are described as looking much like some of the dinosaurs—having large bodies and small heads, and swimming with fins (no legs). There are some pictures of them but no bodies have ever been found.

1. What title would you give this story?

   _____

   _____

2. Using the dictionary, explain what "exist" means.

   _____

   _____

3. Do you think these creatures exist? Explain why/why not.

   _____

   _____

   _____

Name _____

DITTO 144, USING A DICTIONARY

Little children like Teddy Bears. You probably have had one at one time or other. Did you know that real Teddy Bears live in the country of Australia? These lovable, cuddly and friendly animals are called Koalas.

Koalas live in eucalyptus trees. They depend on the leaves of this tree for both food and water. They can often be seen hanging upside down in branches of these Australian trees. Koalas have long toes that help them <u>grasp</u> the branches. During the day, koalas like to sleep.

The mother koala has a pouch and carries her baby in it for several months. When the baby is ready, it will ride on the mother's back.

Until recently, koalas were being killed in large numbers for their wonderfully soft warm fur, but the government has now made it against the law to kill them.

1. What title would you give this story?

   _____

   _____

2. Using a dictionary, tell what "grasp" means.

   _____

   _____

3. In your opinion, should people kill animals for their fur? Explain how you arrived at the

   answer to this question. _____

   _____

   _____

   _____

Name _____

DITTO #145, USING A DICTIONARY

When most people hear the word "dog," they think of some pet. We rarely give credit to the millions of working dogs.

Most of us have at some time encountered a seeing-eye dog dutifully leading its blind owner carefully along a street. But are you aware that there are also hearing-ear dogs for the deaf? These dogs let their owners know when the phone rings or when someone knocks on the door. You may also have seen a police dog on duty acting as a helping partner to the officer. Some police dogs have been specially trained to sniff out drugs.

Search and Rescue groups also use dogs. They can pull drowning people out of the water or locate lost people in rough <u>terrain</u>. Last, we must not forget the teams of dogs who pull sleds across snow-covered lands. All of these working dogs add greatly to the quality of life for the people they serve. They are often true heroes because they save lives. They often put their own lives in jeopardy to help those they serve.

1. What title would you give this story?

   _____

   _____

2. Using a dictionary, explain what "terrain" means.

   _____

   _____

3. What do you think the expression "quality of life" means?

   _____

   _____

   _____

DITTO #146, USING A DICTIONARY

Hundreds of years ago, most people lived in tiny villages. Everyone knew each other and each person had a different name, such as John. As time went on, the villages grew bigger and there was more than one person named John so the need arose to have a way to tell which John was being discussed. People began to say things like John the baker; this person later became known as John Baker. A man who owned the store was called a cooper, thus we might find a John Cooper. The last name of Smith is widespread because in those days there were many men who worked with metals—goldsmiths, silversmiths, and blacksmiths. A blacksmith (who made horse shoes) might call himself John Black or John Smith.

If a man moved from one town to another, he might choose to identify himself by taking the name of the town where he was born, such as John Harwell who came from Harwell, England. The son of a John sometimes gave his last name as Johnson.

Do you know the <u>origin</u> of your family name?

1. What title would you give this story?

   _____

   _____

2. Using a dictionary, explain what "origin" means.

   _____

   _____

3. What do you think John Barber did for a living?

   _____

   _____

   _____

Name _____

DITTO #147, USING A DICTIONARY

If you ever get the <u>opportunity</u> to travel to Venice, Italy, plan to spend several delightful days there. You will arrive outside the city. To get downtown, you must either walk or go by boat.

Venice is built on islands that are connected by a series of footbridges. Waterways called "canals" serve as streets. There are no cars or buses in Venice. By boat, you enter Venice on the Grand Canal. Beautiful palaces and churches—some hundreds of years old—line that canal. Your boat may be as small as the gondola, which carries up to eight people, or as large as the vaporetto—also called the water bus—which carries huge crowds of people. The vaporetto will take you along the larger canals; but to really see Venice properly, you will want to ride with a singing boatman or Gondolier who will take you into the narrow canals that wind through the many islands that make up this city.

Be sure to visit St. Mark's Square with its wonderful outdoor cafes, its large number of pigeons, and its glass and lace shops.

1. What title would you give this story?

   _____

2. Using a dictionary, explain what "opportunity" means.

   _____

   _____

3. The palaces of Venice have garages. What do you think is parked in them?

   _____

   _____

DITTO #148, USING A DICTIONARY

Have you read stories about giants and dwarfs? In stories, these creatures usually have magical powers. In real life we do have people who are classified as giants and dwarfs. If you <u>attain</u> a height over eight feet, you are a giant. If you never get to be four feet tall, doctors call you a dwarf.

Both conditions seem to be caused by disturbances in the amount of hormone produced by the pituitary gland. If the gland produces too much hormone, growth is accelerated. Too little hormone, conversely, may inhibit growth.

The dwarfs, also known as midgets, have formed an organization called the "Little People of America." They get together to have fun and develop job opportunities for dwarfs. If two midgets marry, their children may grow to normal size. When the condition is recognized early, extra hormone can be given.

1. What title would you give this selection?

   _____

   _____

2. Using a dictionary, tell what the word "attain" means.

   _____

   _____

3. If you had to be one or the other, would you choose to be a dwarf or a giant? Tell why.

   _____

   _____

   _____

SYNONYMS

Synonyms are words that have *similar* meanings. A knowledge of them is necessary if a person is to be able to paraphrase what he or she has read. The best way to teach synonyms is to make it a game. Activities that involve only one exposure to the words do not lead to acquisition of the synonyms, so use a game format, called the Synonym Game, that students play every day until they are proficient. Using heavy 18″ x 24″ paper, make game boards that look like this:

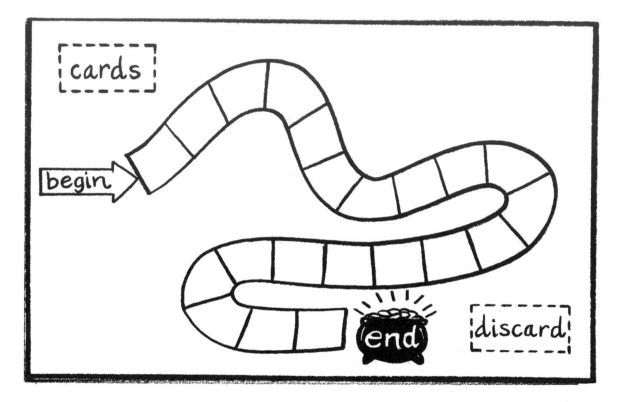

Using 2″ x 3″ cards, put a different underlined word from the word lists on each card. Make a copy of the list you want learned and attach it to a heavy piece of backing paper. Spend several days going over the words until the students can read them.

Three children (two opponents and one referee) can play at each board. Before the game begins, the three people read the entire list. After play begins, only the referee can look at the list. It is his or her job to check the accuracy of the players' answers.

Decide who will play first. Player One draws a card and is allowed to move one space for each correct synonym he or she is able to give for the word on the drawn card. If Player One is able to give all the synonyms for a given word, he or she may take another card. If Player One cannot give all the synonyms for the word, he or she discards and it is Player Two's turn. Play continues until someone reaches the END. The winner then switches place with the referee and a new game begins. (I use lemon drops to encourage play—the winner gets two while the other players get one.)

DITTO #149, SYNONYMS

Word List 1

arrive—come, reach
beautiful—lovely, pretty
beneath—below, under
brook—stream, creek
carry—tote, lug, haul
complete—end, finish
construct—build, make, do
couple—two, pair
depart—leave, go
discover—find, locate
enormous—big, large
entire—all, whole

error—mistake, blunder
frequently—often, repeatedly
important—necessary, needed, essential, useful
join—unite, combine, add
portion—part, piece
reply—response, answer
soil—dirt, ground, earth
toss—throw, pitch, fling

Word List 2

abandon—vacate, desert,
        leave
ailing—sick, ill
amaze—surprise, astonish
arouse—awaken, excite
bother—annoy, pester, irritate,
        aggravate, disturb
bunch—set, group, cluster
choose—pick, select
clutch—grasp, hold
compile—gather, collect,
        accumulate

customary—usual, ordinary
delicate—frail, fragile, weak
destroy—spoil, ruin, trash
eliminate—omit, remove
exhausted—tired, weary
fidget—squirm, wiggle
foolish—silly, stupid, dumb,
        ridiculous
furious—angry, mad
glisten—shine, glow, sparkle
positive—sure, certain
scared—frightened, afraid

Word List 3

ancient—old, aged
anxious—worried, upset,
        nervous
blossom—bloom, flower
boulder—stone, rock
calm—soothe, quiet, still
concept—thought, idea
devour—eat, consume
frolic—play, romp
glance—look, glimpse
high—tall, lofty
increase—gain, grow, accumulate

proper—right, correct
remarked—said, stated
require—need, want
retain—keep, hold
reveal—show, display,
        uncover, disclose
seize—take, grab, hold
single—one, solo, lone
terrible—awful, bad,
        horrible, dreadful
tremble—shake, quake, quiver

Word List 4

account—story, tale
alter—change, very
ample—enough, plenty
        sufficient
arrange—place, put
bellow—yell, scream, shout
commence—begin, start
consider—think, believe,
        study
crave—want, desire
demonstrate—show, display
endeavor—try, attempt, strive

labor—work, toil
minute—tiny, small, little
numerous—many, several
perhaps—maybe, possibly
possess—have, own
question—ask, probe
revolve—twist, turn, spin
saunter—stroll, walk
smart—bright, clever,
        intelligent
summon—call, beckon

Word List 5

argument—quarrel, disagreement
authentic—real, genuine
authorize—permit, allow
beat—pound, hit, strike, pummel
chore—task, job
coax—persuade, convince
damp—wet, moist
dismal—sad, gloomy, dark

fat—plump, obese, stout, husky
garbage—refuse, rubbish, trash
hate—loathe, dislike, despise
junction—crossing, intersection
lean—thin, skinny, slender
plead—beg, implore
promote—advance, progress
primary—first, main, chief
release—extricate, free
summit—top, crest, zenith
trip—journey, expedition, voyage

HARDER ANTONYMS

Antonyms are words that have opposite meanings. The words in this list on Ditto #150 are a bit harder than the ones we've looked at before, but if the students learned the others, they can learn these by practicing them. (See the teaching suggestions in Units 2 and 3 of this book. You will need to explain the meanings of these words and give lots of examples of how to use them.)

DITTO #150, HARDER ANTONYMS

agile—clumsy

animated—sluggish

arrive—depart

bold—shy

calm—nervous

create—destroy

dawn—dusk

dull—shiny

friend—enemy

helpful—harmful

increase—decrease

kind—cruel

knowledge—ignorance

narrow—wide

occupied—vacant

often—seldom

permit—prohibit

problem—solution

shallow—deep

shout—whisper

ugly—beautiful

vague—clear

UNDERSTANDING CAUSE AND EFFECT RELATIONSHIPS

LD students often have difficulty sorting out cause and effect. It is important to talk to them about action and reaction.

I touch the hot stove. Quickly I jerked my hand back.

(action or cause)   **(reaction or effect)**

Another way:

I jerked my hand back because the stove was hot.

(effect)   **(cause)**

When you read sentences of this kind, you have to decide what came first. That is the <u>cause</u>. Whatever happens next is the <u>effect</u>.

In this section you will find Dittoes #151 and 152. It is suggested that these be done as a group with discussion of what is the <u>cause</u> and what is the <u>effect</u>.

ABBREVIATIONS

Ditto #153 is for the students' notebooks. LD students rarely have trouble with abbreviations.

Name _____

DITTO #151, CAUSE AND EFFECT RELATIONSHIPS

Directions: Read each sentence. Ask yourself, "What happened first?" Draw one line under the part that shows cause and draw two lines under the part of the sentence that explains what happened next.

1. The floor was so slippery that she fell.

2. He opened the window because it was so hot in the room.

3. I jumped when the waiter dropped the tray of dishes.

4. When it started to rain, she opened her umbrella.

5. The music was loud and unpleasant so Sam left the room.

6. The cat ran up the tree to get away from the big dog.

7. The teacher said, "Open your books to page 43," so the students got out their books.

8. I ate because I was hungry.

9. The baby was so tired that she fell asleep in her high chair.

10. When he called her "a quitter," she got angry.

11. Mrs. Green smiled at the baby and the baby smiled back.

12. He was ashamed when he got caught cheating.

13. She realized it was cold outside so she put on her mittens and coat.

Name _____

DITTO #152, CAUSE AND EFFECT RELATIONSHIPS

Directions: <u>Read</u> each sentence. <u>Ask yourself,</u> "What happened first?" <u>Draw</u> one line under the part that shows cause and <u>draw</u> two lines under the part of the sentence that explains what happened next.

1. She is such a friendly girl that everyone is her friend.

2. George studied hard and got 100% on the science test.

3. My car hit the one in front of me when the brakes failed.

4. He spit the milk out because it tasted bad.

5. If you are late taking a book back to the library, you will have to pay a fine.

6. She was worried sick when her husband had not come home by 10:00 P.M.

7. I got a speeding ticket for going 50 in a 35-mile zone.

8. She was able to go to Europe because she had saved her money.

9. I have a bruise where I hit my head on the cabinet door.

10. Offended by the gore, she turned off the T.V.

11. The baby was stolen from the car while the mother was in the post office.

12. The sun came out while it was still misting, so a beautiful rainbow could be seen.

13. If he was sassy to his mother, he always got in trouble.

DITTO #153, STUDENT NOTEBOOK HANDOUT, ABBREVIATIONS

Busy people find ways to take shortcuts. Abbreviations represent shortened versions of commonly used words. The lists given here contain only those most frequently used.

afternoon and evening

P.M.

dozen

dz.

Avenue

Ave.

et cetera (and so forth)

etc.

Boulevard

Blvd.

foot

ft.

building

bldg.

gallon

gal.

company

co.

hour

hr.

corporation

corp.

inch

in.

department

Dept.

Junior

Jr.

Doctor of Dental Surgery

Dentist

D.D.S.

miles per hour

m.p.h.

minute

min.

Doctor of Medicine

Dr.

M.D.

morning (midnight til noon)

A.M.

DITTO #153, STUDENT NOTEBOOK HANDOUT,
ABBREVIATIONS, CONTINUED

Mister
Mr.

Mistress (a married woman)
Mrs.

ounce
oz.

paid
pd.

page
pg.

pound
lb.

quart
qt.

Senior
Sr.

Street
St.

week
wk.

yard
yd.

year
yr.

Monday
Mon.

Tuesday
Tues.

Wednesday
Wed.

Thursday
Thurs.

Friday
Fri.

Saturday
Sat.

Sunday
Sun.

January
Jan.

February
Feb.

August
Aug.

September
Sept.

October
Oct.

November
Nov.

December
Dec.

Name _____

DITTO #153, STUDENT NOTEBOOK HANDOUT, ABBREVIATIONS CONTINUED

Alabama	AL	Nebraska	NE
Alaska	AK	Nevada	NV
Arizona	AZ	New Hampshire	NH
Arkansas	AR	New Jersey	NJ
		New Mexico	NM
California	CA	New York	NY
Colorado	CO	North Carolina	NC
Connecticut	CT	North Dakota	ND
Delaware	DE	Ohio	OH
Florida	FL	Oklahoma	OK
Georgia	GA	Oregon	OR
Hawaii	HI		
		Pennsylvania	PA
Idaho	ID	Rhode Island	RI
Illinois	IL		
Indiana	IN	South Carolina	SC
Iowa	IA	South Dakota	SD
Kansas	KS	Tennessee	TN
Kentucky	KY	Texas	TX
Louisiana	LA	Utah	UT
		Vermont	VT
Maine	ME	Virginia	VA
Maryland	MD		
Massachusetts	MA	Washington	WA
Michigan	MI	West Virginia	WV
Minnesota	MN	Wisconsin	WI
Missouri	MO		
Montana	MT	District of Columbia	D.C.

WORDS WITH MULTIPLE MEANINGS

Our language is full of words that have multiple meanings. When students reach a functional level of third grade, they are ready to be systematically exposed to them. The list on Ditto #154 is suggested—it does not represent a full listing. Students will use Ditto # 154 to do #155 and #156.

DITTO #154, WORDS WITH MULTIPLE MEANINGS

arms 1. part of the upper body; 2. weapons

bank 1. a place for keeping your money; 2. a mound of dirt

bark 1. the skin of a tree; 2. the sound a dog makes

bill 1. a demand for money owed; 2. beak on a bird

bit 1. a small piece; 2. a tool for drilling; 3. past tense of bite

bore 1. to make a hole; 2. to carry; 3. dull and uninteresting

can 1. to be able to do; 2. a metal container

clip 1. to cut; 2. to fasten

close 1. to shut; 2. to be near

desert 1. a dry barren place; 2. to leave

fair 1. plays by the rules; 2. bazaar/exhibit; 3. lovely; 4. average; 5. light in color; 6. clear

fine 1. high quality; 2. money paid as punishment

fire 1. flames; 2. to excite; 3. to lose a job for cause

fit 1. suitable; 2. right size or shape; 3. put in place; 4. sudden attack

grave 1. a place of burial; 2. important or serious

hatch 1. the birth of an animal from an egg; 2. an opening in a ship's deck

hide 1. to conceal out of sight; 2. an animal's skin

kind 1. classify by sort; 2. helpful, gentle, understanding

lap 1. a body part formed when you sit; 2. to drink using the tongue; 3. a distance traveled

lie 1. to tell a falsehood; 2. to recline for rest

like 1. to be similar; 2. to be pleased with

loaf 1. to be idle, not working; 2. the shape of bread

mine 1. belonging to me; 2. a hole in the Earth from which ores such as gold, silver, and coal are removed; 3. an explosive

rest 1. to relax or sleep; 2. the portion that is left

row 1. line; 2. to use oars to make a boat move

saw 1. did see; 2. a tool for cutting

soil 1. to get dirty; 2. earth or ground

spell 1. to write or say the letters in a word; 2. a period of time; 3. a magic influence

stall 1. a place to keep a horse; 2. to delay; 3. when a motor suddenly stops working

DITTO #155, WORDS WITH MULTIPLE MEANINGS, ACTIVITY SHEET

Directions: <u>Read</u> each sentence. From your list of words with multiple meanings, <u>choose</u> the meaning that fits in the sentence. <u>Rewrite the sentence</u> on the back of this sheet substituting the meaning for the word.

1. With the end of the war, both sides reduced their <u>arms</u> supply.

2. We ran to the top of the <u>bank</u> to see the view of the desert.

3. The <u>bark</u> of the oak is very rough.

4. The <u>bill</u> of a sea gull allows it to catch fish.

5. May I try a <u>bit</u> of that chocolate pie?

6. The electric drill can <u>bore</u> a hole quickly.

7. Inspect the <u>can</u> to make sure it is not damaged.

8. The barber began to <u>clip</u> the hair from around my ears.

9. Inside the dark cave, stay <u>close</u> to me.

10. We will not <u>desert</u> you while you are still ill.

11. We saw many interesting things at the <u>fair</u>.

12. The <u>fine</u> for parking in the blue zone was $50.

13. The belt was not a good <u>fit</u>.

14. If I am late, I might be <u>fired</u>.

Name _____

DITTO #156, WORDS WITH MULTIPLE MEANINGS, ACTIVITY SHEET

Directions: <u>Read</u> each sentence. Using your list of words with multiple meanings, decide what you think the word means by the context of the sentence. <u>Rewrite the sentence</u> on the back of this sheet substituting the meaning you chose for the word.

1. The doctor wore a <u>grave</u> look as he spoke of my aunt's illness.

2. We watched as the egg <u>hatched.</u>

3. The cow's <u>hide</u> was used for making purses and shoes.

4. My grandpa is a <u>kind</u> old man.

5. The thirsty dog began to eagerly <u>lap</u> water from his bowl.

6. He didn't want to be spanked so the boy told a <u>lie</u>.

7. I <u>like</u> the dress you bought very much.

8. Since he lost his job, all he did was <u>loaf</u>.

9. That book is <u>mine</u>.

10. If you don't eat your whole steak, save the <u>rest</u> for me.

11. There are five <u>rows</u> of desks in the room.

12. I <u>saw</u> him do it with my own two eyes!

13. He dropped two seeds in the top of each mound of <u>soil</u>.

14. We have had a long hot <u>spell</u> this summer.

15. The car <u>stalled</u> right in the middle of the intersection.

Words That Describe Feelings

One of the areas of deficit we often see in children with learning disabilities is an extremely limited repertory of words that let us know how a person feels. After reading a passage, if you ask the question "How does _____ feel?" the student almost always will say "good" or "bad."

Ditto #157 is a list you may refer to in helping students build their vocabularies.

I have used a technique called "Word for the Day" in dealing with this subject. Each day choose one word that you will work on—students try to learn to spell it, know what it means, find an example of it in their reading or daily life, role-play how a person looks or acts when feeling this emotion, and put it on an ongoing list in the student notebook. If you can find a way to give bonus points for using the words in later lessons, it can almost feel like a game.

Each day, add a new word and review the old words. By Friday there are five words; on the following Monday, drop the first word from the daily review so that the daily review list always has no more than five words. You may, however, want to put up a bulletin board or a strip of butcher paper and keep a running list so that the words are not out of sight and students can always refer back to them. Also feel free to add other emotions. The ones given here are just a starter list; make the list relevant to your students' reading or writing needs.

These lessons offer opportunities to discuss how we can handle these natural feelings. For students who come from dysfunctional situations, this may become very therapeutic. For example, anger is a feeling we all must deal with. There are times we must be assertive and talk directly with the person who made us mad; other times we must learn to find a release for that anger but cannot deal directly with the person or situation that makes us angry. Role-playing can be very beneficial if you help students practice how to be assertive without offending.

DITTO #157, WORDS THAT DESCRIBE FEELINGS

happy	curious	lost
gleeful	suspicious	forlorn
joyous	anxious	lonesome
contented	worried	homesick
elated	upset	
	uneasy	bashful
sad/blue	frantic	shy
depressed		timid
gloomy	mad	
	angry	ashamed
amazed	aggravated	guilty
startled	irritated	
surprised	furious	bored
stunned	exasperated	disinterested
shocked	annoyed	inattentive
	cross	
scared	grouchy	indignant
afraid		offended
frightened	excited	
terrified	eager	confident
horrified	agitated	satisfied
fearful	fidgety	pleased
dread	frustrated	proud
dismayed	tired	defeated
puzzled	weary	discouraged
confused	sleepy	
perplexed	drowsy	awed
	exhausted	overwhelmed

Signal Words

As students write they will encounter the need for signal words. These are words that indicate spatial direction, sequence, time passage, a change of direction, or additional ideas.

Ditto #158 gives a partial listing of some of the most common signal words. Students will want a copy of these for their notebooks.

DITTO #158, STUDENT NOTEBOOK HANDOUT, SIGNAL WORDS

Spatial Direction

up	between	left
down	by	right
here	center	diagonally
there	middle	horizontally
near	across	vertically
far	over	behind
east	below	front
west	under	back
north	inside	beyond
south	outside	top
adjacent	away	bottom

Sequence

first	next	then
second	finally	last
third		

Time Direction

earlier	before	until
later	after	still
during	since	now
while		

Words That Indicate a Change of Direction

on the contrary	but	conversely
on the other hand	unless	
in contrast	otherwise	

Words That Indicate Additional Ideas Are Coming

and	for example	also
so	for instance	specifically
thus	furthermore	such as
because	therefore	hence
consequently		

HOMOPHONES

Homophones are words that sound the same, but have different meanings and spellings. The lists on Ditto #159 are by no means complete, but represent ones encountered often. Students will use Ditto #159 to do Ditto #163

Dittoes #160 through 163 are activity sheets to go with this section and may be done as class seatwork or homework. You will need to explain the meaning of the word "obliterate" and demonstrate what students are to do.

DITTO #159, STUDENT NOTEBOOK HANDOUT, HOMOPHONES

ad (advertisement)

add (combining sets)

allowed (permitted)

aloud (voiced)

ant (insect)

aunt (the sister of your mother or father)

ate (swallow food)

eight (number)

bare (naked or empty)

bear (animal)

berry (fruit)

bury (put in the ground)

blew (did blow)

blue (color)

board (wood)

bored (without interest)

brake (to stop)

break (destroy)

buy (to purchase)

by (near or beside)

ceiling (top of the room)

sealing (to close)

chews (to gnash food)

choose (to select)

close (to shut)

clothes (things you wear)

die (end life)

dye (tint/color)

DITTO #159, STUDENT NOTEBOOK HANDOUT, HOMOPHONES, CONTINUED

find (to locate)

fined (money penalty)

flea (insect)

flee (to run away)

flour (ground grain)

flower (blossom)

for (given to)

fore (front part)

four (number)

groan (a noise)

grown (to grow)

heal (to make well)

heel (back of foot)

he'll (he will)

hear (listen)

here (place)

hole (cavity)

whole (all or entire)

hour (60 minutes)

our (it belongs to us)

know (recognize)

no (negative)

made (to construct)

maid (a servant)

mail (to send)

male (boys or men)

one (number)

won (to win)

pair (two or couple)

pare (to peel)

pear (fruit)

pause (a brief stop)

paws (animal feet)

peace (quiet, calm)

piece (part)

right (correct)

write (make marks)

their (it belongs to them)

there (place)

they're (they are)

sea (ocean)

see (visualize)

waist (middle of the body)

waste (trash)

soar (to fly)

sore (painful)

way (a path or route)

weigh (measure heaviness)

son (male offspring)

sun (star)

weak (without strength)

week (seven days)

to (toward)

too (also)

wood (forest or from a tree)

two (pair)

would (past tense of will)

Name _____

DITTO #160, HOMOPHONES, ACTIVITY SHEET

Directions: <u>Read</u> each sentence. From your list of homophones, <u>choose</u> the word that fits the sentence. <u>Obliterate</u> the word that does not fit the meaning of the sentence. Your teacher will explain what "obliterate" means.

1. When Nancy's cat disappeared, she put an <u>ad add</u> in the newspaper offering a reward for its return.

2. I am not <u>allowed aloud</u> to watch T.V. for more than one hour a day.

3. My <u>ant aunt</u> and uncle are coming for a visit.

4. Mother cut the pie into <u>ate eight</u> slices.

5. When I realized the cupboards and refrigerator were <u>bare bear</u>, I knew it was time to go to the grocery store.

6. Our dog likes to dig. He will <u>berry bury</u> bones and toys.

7. The wind <u>blew blue</u> the man's hat off.

8. Dad used the saw to cut the <u>board bored</u> into two parts.

9. Be careful with those dishes. They <u>brake break</u> easily.

10. We looked at new cars but we did not <u>buy by</u> one.

Name _____

DITTO #161, HOMOPHONES, ACTIVITY SHEET

Directions: <u>Read</u> each sentence. From the list of homophones, <u>choose</u> the word that fits the sentence. <u>Obliterate</u> the word that does not belong. Your teacher will explain what "obliterate" means.

1. The <u>ceiling sealing</u> of the church was covered with beautiful pictures.

2. When you <u>chews choose</u> a career, pick one you will enjoy.

3. Mother gets angry if I do not hang my <u>close clothes</u>.

4. The curtains had faded so I decided to <u>die dye</u> them.

5. The teacher could not <u>find fined</u> her keys.

6. I saw a <u>flea flee</u> run across my dog's tummy.

7. Mother cut the <u>flour flower</u> and put it in a vase.

8. This package is <u>for fore</u> you.

9. When I hit my thumb with the hammer, it made me <u>groan grown</u>.

10. The shoes caused a blister on my <u>heel he'll</u>.

Name _____

DITTO #162, HOMOPHONES, ACTIVITY SHEET

Directions: <u>Read</u> each sentence. From the list of homophones, <u>choose</u> the word that fits the meaning of the sentence. <u>Obliterate</u> the word that does not belong. Your teacher will explain what "obliterate" means.

1. Can you <u>hear here</u> that faint ticking noise?

2. Jon ate the <u>hole whole</u> pizza by himself.

3. Each class is about an <u>hour our</u> long.

4. She said she would <u>know no</u> the thief if she ever saw him again.

5. Mrs. Brown decided to hire a <u>made maid</u> to do her housework.

6. Until recently, only <u>mail male</u> pilots could fly in combat.

7. When he learned he had <u>one won</u> the prize, he jumped for joy.

8. That is a good-looking <u>pair pare</u> of shoes you bought.

9. Your new dog certainly has huge <u>pause paws</u>.

10. When my Dad is home, he likes <u>peace piece</u> and quiet.

Name _____

DITTO # 163, HOMOPHONES ACTIVITY SHEET

Directions: Read each sentence. From your list of homophones, choose the word that fits the meaning of the sentence. Obliterate the word that does not belong. Your teacher will explain what "obliterate" means.

1. Be sure to right write your name on your paper.

2. From reading the directions, can you sea see how this is going to work?

3. After working out at the gym, his muscles were soar sore.

4. Their son sun is a fighter jet pilot in the navy.

5. Mike is going to the store. May I go, to too?

6. Did you know that their they're twins?

7. Put that junk in the waist waste basket, please.

8. I way weigh myself every day to be sure I am not getting thinner.

9. He lost so much blood, he felt weak week.

10. We have cut down so many trees that wood would is costly.

PREFIXES, ROOTS, AND SUFFIXES

Many of today's words had their beginning in earlier languages. A knowledge of the ancient Greek and Roman languages is helpful in understanding what words mean. It is important for children to know that language is not static and new words are constantly being added to the dictionary. Likewise, words drop out of usage as well.

In teaching this section you might liken it to a train. Let the engine represent the Prefix, a boxcar represent the Root, and the caboose represent the Suffix. A bulletin board display might look like this:

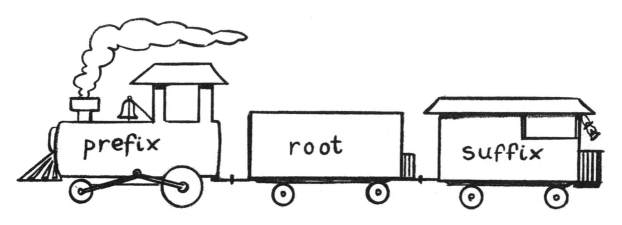

Give each student copies of Dittoes #164 through 166 to place in their notebooks for future reference. The lists given here are not complete, but they are sufficient to allow students to get a basic feel for how these word-parts function together. Everything necessary to complete the activity sheets is on the lists.

Dittoes #167 through 172 seem better received when students are allowed to work on them in pairs, cooperatively. Do not introduce this topic until a student has a functional reading level of about 4.0. If you decide to use the sheets earlier than that, you will need to help students read and complete them.

Try to make doing the activities fun. Heap praise on pairs who complete them. Small edible rewards, allowing students to play their music quietly while working, giving a bit of help here and there, displaying papers that are completed, sending a note home—all of these make the task more pleasant.

DITTO #164, STUDENT NOTEBOOK HANDOUT, PREFIXES

ab—away from

acro—high

ad—to

an—not

anti—against

ast—star

auto—self

bene—good

bi—two

circu—around

co—together/with

col—together/with

com—together/with

con—together/with

contra—against

counter—against

de—down

dia—across

en—in

ex—out

extra—outside

hyper—too much

hypo—under/too little

il—not

im—into

im—not

in—into

in—not

inter—between

intro—inside

micro—small

mis—bad

mono—one

multi—many

omni—all

peri—around

poly—many

post—after

pre—before

pro—forward

quadri—four

re—again

retro—back

sub—under

sym—together

syn—together

tele—distant

trans—across

tri—three

un—not

DITTO #165, STUDENT NOTEBOOK HANDOUT, ROOTS

© 1995 by The Center for Applied Research in Education

act—do

aero—air

anthr—man

aqua—water

arch—chief

audi—hear

belli—war

bio—life

cede—go

ceed—go

cert—sure

chron—time

cide—kill

cise—cut

claim—shout

cline—lean

clude—shut

cogn—know

cur—care

cycl—ring/circle

derm—skin

dict—speak

donat—give

duct—lead

fac—make

flect—bend

flex—bend

fract—break

frag—break

geo—land

gnos—know

gon—angle

grad—step

gram—letter

graph—write

gress—step

here—stick

hom—man

ject—throw

lab—work

lat—side

liber—free

lit—read

lith—stone

loc—place

log—word

lum—light

man—hand

mand—order

marine—water

mater—mother

max—greatest

merge—dive

meter—measure

min—small

mob—move

mot—move

nat—born

neo—new

opt—eye

pater—father

ped—foot

philo—love

phono—sound

pod—foot

poli—city

port—carry

quer—ask

ques—ask

rupt—break

scend—climb

scribe—write

script—written

sect—cut

spect—look

strict—tight

tain—hold

terr—land

therm—heat

tract—pull/drag

urb—city

vac—empty

vag—wander

ver—truth

vid—see

vis—see

volv—turn

vor—eat

DITTO #166, STUDENT NOTEBOOK HANDOUT, SUFFIXES

study of—nom
  nomy
  ology

full of—ful
  ous

less—without

one who/person who—
  ant
  arian
  ent
  er
  ist
  or

act of/state of—
  ism
  ive
  ment
  tion
  ure

place for—arium
  orium

able to—able
  ible

to make—ate
  en
  fy
  ize

fear of—phobia

Name _____

DITTO #167, PREFIX—ROOT—SUFFIX, ACTIVITY SHEET

bio	logy	neo	natal	tele	phone	aqua	phobia

(_____)(_____)   (_____)(_____)   (_____)(_____)   (_____)(_____)

bi	ped	rupt	ure	pre	dict	spect	a	tor

(_____)(_____)   (_____)(_____)   (_____)(_____)   (_____) (_____)

hypo	act	ive	ver	dict

(_____)(_____)(_____)   (_____)(_____)

Using the prefix—root—suffix lists, put the meaning of each word part within the parentheses provided above. Then use the words in the sentences below, letting the context of each sentence guide you.

1. In __ __ __ __ __ __ __ we study about the body's life-sustaining organs.

2. After nearly drowning, she developed __ __ __ __ __ __ __ __ __ __.

3. The invention of the __ __ __ __ __ __ __ __ __ allows us to talk with people around the world.

4. The babies are placed in the __ __ __ __ __ __ __ __ nursery soon after they are born.

5. Rising from his seat, the __ __ __ __ __ __ __ __ __ began to cheer for his team.

6. The human animal is a __ __ __ __ __ who can move very quietly.

7. After looking at the dark clouds and seeing the wind blowing the trees to and fro, Mother

    was able to __ __ __ __ __ __ __ it would rain soon.

8. We saw the volcano __ __ __ __ __ __ __ and the lava come spewing out.

9. The jury reached a __ __ __ __ __ __ __ after listening to all the evidence.

10. The __ __ __ __ __ __ __ __ __ __ child did not feel like playing because she felt tired all the time.

Name _____

DITTO #168, PREFIX—ROOT—SUFFIX, ACTIVITY SHEET

in   spect   audi to rium   port   able   geo   logy

(_____)(_____)   (_____) (_____)   (_____)(_____)   (_____)(_____)

man u fac ture   bi cycle   sub marine   de scend

(_____) (_____)(_____)   (_____)(_____)   (_____)(_____)   (_____)(_____)

ex   claimed   astro nom   er

(_____)(_____)   (_____)(_____)(_____)

Using the prefix—root—suffix lists, put the meaning of each word part within the parentheses provided above. Then use the words in the sentences below, letting the context of each sentence guide you.

1. Be careful when you ascend and _ _ _ _ _ _ _ from a ladder.

2. The _ _ _ _ _ _ _ _ _ _ _ _ was built in such a way that you can hear everything that is said on the stage, no matter where you sit.

3. In our _ _ _ _ _ _ _ _ class, we studied how the Earth began and we learned a lot about rocks.

4. The child took the _ _ _ _ _ _ _ _ TV into his room.

5. A _ _ _ _ _ _ _ has only two wheels.

6. At the airport, a guard will _ _ _ _ _ _ _ your bag before allowing it to be put on the airplane.

7. The new building will house a business that will _ _ _ _ _ _ _ _ _ _ _ _ dolls with hand-painted faces.

8. The _ _ _ _ _ _ _ _ _ _ turned his telescope toward the large bright star he saw in the evening sky.

9. The _ _ _ _ _ _ _ _ _ is a kind of boat that can dive under the water and travel beneath the water.

10. "Fire!" she _ _ _ _ _ _ _ _ _.

Name _____

DITTO #169, PREFIX—ROOT—SUFFIX, ACTIVITY SHEET

ex   port   acro   phobia   mani   cure   tri   pod

(_____)(_____)   (_____)(_____)   (_____)(_____)   (_____)(_____)

aqua   rium   flex   ible   dia   meter   pro   spect

(_____)(_____)   (_____)(_____)   (_____)(_____)   (_____)(_____)

contra   dict   micro   scope

(_____)(_____)   (_____)(_____)

Using the prefix—root—suffix lists, put the meaning of each word part in the parentheses provided above. Then use the words in the sentence below, letting the context of each sentence guide you.

1. Animals with only one cell are so small that you must have a

   _ _ _ _ _ _ _ _ _ _ to see them.

2. When my nails are all torn and broken, I give myself a _ _ _ _ _ _ _ _.

3. The board was cut very thin so it would be _ _ _ _ _ _ _ _ and could be used to go around the flower beds.

4. We are excited at the _ _ _ _ _ _ _ _ of the baby which is due in about a month.

5. Japan's largest _ _ _ _ _ _ are the cars it sells all over the world.

6. The _ _ _ _ _ _ _ _ had windows so we could look at the many kinds of fish swimming in natural-like settings.

7. It really makes me angry when you _ _ _ _ _ _ _ _ _ _ what I say.

8. He got a three-legged stand called a _ _ _ _ _ _ so he could put his camera on it and take pictures without worrying about moving the camera.

9. The _ _ _ _ _ _ _ _ of that circle is exactly four inches.

10. People with _ _ _ _ _ _ _ _ _ _ sometimes refuse to go on airplanes.

Name _____

DITTO #170, PREFIX—ROOT—SUFFIX, ACTIVITY SHEET

pro   ject   tele   scope   ped i cure   trans   port

(_____)(_____)   (_____)(_____)   (_____) (_____)   (_____)(_____)

therm o meter   aud   ible   homi   cide   auto   graph

(_____) (_____)   (_____)(_____)   (_____)(_____)   (_____)(_____)

bene   fact   or   retro spect

(_____)(_____)(_____)   (_____)(_____)

Using the prefix—root—suffix lists, write the meaning of each word part in the parentheses provided above. Then use the words in the sentences below, allowing the context of each sentence to guide you.

1. Police investigate all __ __ __ __ __ __ __ __ cases and try to locate the murderers.

2. Using a __ __ __ __ __ __ __ __ __ __ , Jon was able to see more stars than he could with the naked eye.

3. We asked for the actor's __ __ __ __ __ __ __ __ __ on our program.

4. When you act on a stage, you must __ __ __ __ __ __ __ your voice so the audience can hear you.

5. The __ __ __ __ __ __ __ __ __ __ provided a home for the orphans.

6. When you are sick, you need a __ __ __ __ __ __ __ __ __ __ __ to see if you have a fever.

7. When your fingernails are a mess, you may want to get a manicure. When your toenails

   are a mess, you go for a __ __ __ __ __ __ __ __.

8. In __ __ __ __ __ __ __ __ __ __ I realized I could have avoided the accident had I not been following the car ahead of me so closely.

9. She hiccuped so quietly that it was not __ __ __ __ __ __ __.

10. Large ships, called freighters, __ __ __ __ __ __ __ __ __ goods to other countries.

Name _____

DITTO #171, PREFIX—ROOT—SUFFIX, ACTIVITY SHEET

don   ation   ad   here   ex   clude   peri   meter

(_____)(_____)   (_____)(_____)   (_____)(_____)   (_____)(_____)

counter   act   sub   terranean   mon   arch   il   lit   erate

(_____)(_____)   (_____)(_____)   (_____)(_____)   (_____) (_____)

anony   mous   intro   spec   tion

(_____)(_____)   (_____)(_____)(_____)

Using the prefix—root—suffix lists, write the meaning for each word part in the parentheses provided above. Then use the words in the sentences below, allowing the context of each sentence to guide you.

1. The cave was a large _ _ _ _ _ _ _ _ _ _ _ _ one made by the ocean waves.

2. For many years, England had a _ _ _ _ _ _ _ or king who had great power.

3. That tape is so sticky that it will _ _ _ _ _ _ to anything.

4. We had to measure the _ _ _ _ _ _ _ _ _ of the football field by walking all the way around it.

5. When he called "We Tip" to report the crime, he was afraid so he said he wanted to

   remain _ _ _ _ _ _ _ _ _.

6. Drinking milk, water or almost any other fluid won't _ _ _ _ _ _ _ _ poison, but it will allow you more time to get to a hospital.

7. The dyslexic student worked hard so he would not grow up to be

   _ _ _ _ _ _ _ _ _ _.

8. The girls decided to _ _ _ _ _ _ _ boys and have an all-girl party.

9. After much _ _ _ _ _ _ _ _ _ _ _ _ _ _ she decided she was at fault and should apologize.

10. A _ _ _ _ _ _ _ _ of $100 will feed 25 hungry people at the Salvation Army Shelter.

Name _____

DITTO #172, PREFIX—ROOT—SUFFIX, ACTIVITY SHEET

acro   polis   auto   mobile   port   er   labor a   tory

(_____)(_____)   (_____)(_____)   (_____)(_____)   (_____)   (_____)

counter   mand   inter   rupt   lum   i   nous   pro   ceed

(_____)(_____)   (_____)(_____)   (_____)   (_____)   (_____)(_____)

auto   bio   graphy   quadri   lat   er   al

(_____)(_____)(_____)   (_____)(_____)   (_____)

Using the prefix—root—suffix lists, write the meaning of each word part in the parentheses provided above. Then use the words in the sentences below, allowing the context of each sentence to guide you.

1. He was looking forward to retirement so he could write his

   _ _ _ _ _ _ _ _ _ _ _ _ _ describing the events he remembered vividly.

2. You can _ _ _ _ _ _ _ to the next grade.

3. They removed the single light and replaced it with a _ _ _ _ _ _ _ _ ceiling.

4. Because it is a long way to work and bus service was poor, he needed an

   _ _ _ _ _ _ _ _ _ .

5. These suitcases are heavy, so let's get a _ _ _ _ _ _ to put them on the plane.

6. A square is an example of a _ _ _ _ _ _ _ _ _ _ _ _ _ _ .

7. If you _ _ _ _ _ _ _ _ _ our conversation again, you will have to leave.

8. A general has the power to _ _ _ _ _ _ _ _ _ _ _ the captain's order.

9. All the workers in the _ _ _ _ _ _ _ _ _ _ were busy.

10. The ancient Greeks often built their cities atop the highest hill which they called an

   _ _ _ _ _ _ _ _ .

HELPING STUDENTS LEARN CAPITALIZATION/PUNCTUATION RULES

In the early grades, teachers often start the day by putting two or three sentences on the board for students to copy. At the end of each sentence is a number in parentheses telling how many errors there are in the sentence. Students try to find the mistakes and correct them. While they are doing that activity, the teacher has time to take roll and get those early morning details settled. Next, the teacher goes over each sentence asking students to tell *why* a given word is capitalized or why a given punctuation mark is used. This familiarizes students with the rules. *One caution*: Students may fall in the habit of not doing the corrections and just waiting for the teacher to put the answers on the board. You may want to quickly circulate before putting up the answers.

By fourth grade, students can be grouped in pairs or groups of four. A writing assignment is given and the students are instructed to have each member of their group read their paper and critique what needs to be changed. The partners also help if a sentence does not make sense. Sometimes the writing lesson is preceded by a short review of a single concept, such as going over when commas are appropriate.

Dittoes #173 through 175 offer you student notebook handouts and a practice sheet.

The basic reason we use punctuation is to make our written expression as much like our oral expression as possible. The *period, question mark,* and *exclamation point* signal the end of a complete thought. We aim to have the habit of using these in place by the end of grade 3. Other punctuation marks are probably best taught as the student has a need for them in his or her written expression.

DITTO #173, STUDENT NOTEBOOK HANDOUT, CAPITALIZATION RULES

1. Always capitalize the pronoun I.

2. Capitalize the first word of every sentence.

3. Capitalize names of:
   a. specific people
   b. specific places
   c. months
   d. days
   e. documents
   f. titles of articles, books, stories
   g. specific companies or organizations
   h. titles, such as Mr. and Dr.
   i. names of languages, religions, deities

4. Capitalize the first word of a direct quote.

DITTO #174, STUDENT NOTEBOOK HANDOUT, PUNCTUATION RULES

Period   Use a period   (1) at end of a statement.
                                            (2) after initials or abbreviations.

Question Mark   Use the question mark after an inquiry (see list of words that signal questions). You can tell when a question has been asked because a question illicits an answer.

Exclamation Mark   Use an exclamation mark with statements that indicate great emotion or screaming.

Comma   Use a comma   (1) in dates

                                            January 12, 1996

                                            (2) to separate city from state

                                            Los Angeles, California

                                            (3) to separate words or phrases in a series

                                            MaryLou, Jo, and Ann are sisters.

                                            Do your homework, then your chores, and then

                                            you can play.

                                            (4) to set off quotations

                                            Dad said, "Hurry up."

                                            (5) when addressing someone by name

                                            Sherrie, please feed the dog.

                                            Dear Jason,

                                            (6) in closing letters

                                            Sincerely,

Apostrophe   Use the apostrophe (1) to indicate a letter is missing in a contraction

                                            was not becomes wasn't

                                            (2) to show ownership

                                            That is Jon's hat.

Quotation Marks   Use quotation marks to show the exact words of the speaker.

                      The teacher said "Be quiet."

Parentheses   Use parentheses   (1) when you want to insert more information

                                            Get the liter size (33 oz.).

                                            (2) to enumerate choices

                                            You may have (a) soup and sandwich or (b)

                                            salad and sandwich.

Note: Use of the colon and semi-colon are not covered here.

DITTO #175, CAPITALIZATION/PUNCTUATION, PRACTICE SHEET

1. my favorite T.V. show is i love lucy **(5)**

2. we planted tomatoes brussel sprouts and corn in our garden **(4)**

1. christmas always falls on december 25th **(3)**

2. can you help me **(2)**

1. thanksgiving always comes on the last thursday in november **(4)**

2. is mrs smith a good teacher **(5)**

1. the bible is the most read book in the world **(3)**

2. my three sisters are Jan Jill and ann **(5)**

1. the rainbow has six colors—purple blue green yellow orange and red **(7)**

2. did you see the rainbow on sunday **(3)**

1. for many years i lived in new york city **(6)**

2. may i see your book **(3)**

1. have you read a book called charlotte's web **(4)**

2. we had a hamburger potatoes salad and a drink for lunch **(4)**

1. the best book i have read is the secret garden **(6)**

2. how old are you **(2)**

UNDERSTANDING SINGULAR AND PLURAL FORMS OF NOUNS

There are many people who are not sure about the rules for changing a noun to its plural form, although it is rather easy. Ditto #176 gives a list of them. The best way to teach this is to have the students read it over chorally once each day. Then put six words on the board and have the students write the plurals to show they can apply the rules. After they do that, orally go over their answers so they can correct their own papers. Here are some lists of words you may want to use for this purpose:

1. clown	1. dress	1. egg	1. nose	1. calf
2. wolf	2. house	2. knife	2. money	2. glass
3. ranch	3. brush	3. tomato	3. lunch	3. penny
4. grass	4. lady	4. cross	4. heart	4. tire
5. candy	5. hat	5. fox	5. thief	5. tax
6. rooster	6. bunch	6. witch	6. wish	6. guess

UNDERSTANDING PARTS OF SPEECH

Most school districts provide material for teaching parts of speech. In grade 2, they introduce nouns and review them each year thereafter. In grade 3, they introduce verbs and adjectives and review them every year thereafter. By the end of grade 6, each part of speech has been introduced. (See Ditto #177.)

DITTO #176, STUDENT NOTEBOOK HANDOUT, SINGULAR/PLURAL NOUNS

You will remember that <u>a noun is a person, place or thing</u>. We have <u>singular nouns</u> that refer to one person, one place or one thing and we have <u>plural nouns</u> that refer to more than one. For example:

Singular   noun   =   girl   Plural   noun   =   gir<u>ls</u>

Rule: For most nouns we make the plural by adding an <u>s</u>.

     tree becomes tre<u>es</u>   room becomes room<u>s</u>

Exception 1: When a word ends in <u>s</u>, <u>x</u>, <u>o</u>, <u>sh</u>, or <u>ch</u>, you make the plural by adding <u>es</u>. For example:

     bu<u>s</u> becomes bus<u>es</u>   bo<u>x</u> becomes box<u>es</u>   potat<u>o</u> becomes potato<u>es</u>

     di<u>sh</u> becomes dish<u>es</u>   bran<u>ch</u> becomes branch<u>es</u>

Exception 2: With some words that end in <u>f</u> or <u>fe</u>, the plural is made when <u>you change the f to v and then add es</u>. For example:

     lea<u>f</u> becomes lea<u>ves</u>   wi<u>fe</u> becomes wi<u>ves</u>

Exception 3: For words that end in <u>y</u>, the plural is made when <u>you change the y to i and then add es</u>. For example:

     bab<u>y</u> becomes bab<u>ies</u>   lad<u>y</u> becomes lad<u>ies</u>

DITTO #177, STUDENT NOTEBOOK HANDOUT, PARTS OF SPEECH

In English, we have patterns of word usage we call syntax. These patterns determine how we construct sentences. Within a sentence, all words can be classified into eight parts of speech by the way they are used. Here is a chart to help you recall them.

Noun Name of person, place, thing, or idea. *Examples:* the President, mother, O'Hare Airport, Brooklyn Bridge, shirt, bird, beauty, happiness	**Pronoun** Word we use in place of a noun. *Examples:* he, she, it, you, them, we, us, himself, someone
Verbs Word that shows action. *Examples:* run, sing, sleep Words that show being. *Examples:* am, is, are, were	**Adjective** Word that describes a noun. *Examples:* green, huge, American, two, this, third
Adverb Word that describes a verb. *Examples:* quietly, thoughtfully, too	**Conjunction** Word that is used to join words or a group of words. *Examples:* and, but, so
Preposition Word that shows relationship of a noun/pronoun to another word. *Examples:* by, during, toward	**Interjection** Word that expresses great emotion. *Examples:* Oops! Bravo! Cool!

How Authors Use Words to Paint Pictures/The Role of Adjectives

Adjectives are words that tell or describe how things look, feel, sound, and taste. These words help us paint a mental picture to go with what we are reading. To illustrate these ideas to students, put this sentence on the board:

The woman placed a hat on her head.

Have students read the statement, then ask, **"How old was this woman? What color was her hair? What did the hat look like?"**

Students will see they do not have a clear picture of the woman. Now rewrite the sentence:

The elderly woman placed a wide-brimmed, red hat on her head.

Point out to students how the word <u>elderly</u> changes our concept of the woman and how the words <u>wide-brimmed</u> and <u>red</u> help us see the hat.) Rewrite the sentence:

The pretty young woman placed a flowered hat on her head.

After students read the sentence they will revise their mental picture. Explain to them that words that describe the woman and her hat are examples of adjectives.

Here's a second example:

The path led us up to the mountain meadow where a deer could be seen feeding on the grasses.

The <u>winding, rocky</u> path led us up to the <u>high</u> mountain meadow where a <u>dozen</u> deer could be seen feeding on the <u>tall</u> grasses.

The <u>steep, dirt</u> path led us up to the <u>large</u> mountain meadow where a <u>great buck</u> deer could be seen feeding on the <u>spring-green</u> grasses.

You also need to show students how adjectives can be used to paint a picture of a sound:

A <u>shrill, ear-piercing</u> siren told us the ambulance was here.

Adjectives also help us taste:

The iced tea was <u>sour</u> until I put two spoonfuls of sugar in it.

Here is an example of how adjectives can be used to describe feelings:

The losers congratulated the winners but in their minds they felt very <u>dejected</u> over their defeat.

For practice in developing an awareness of the role of adjectives, take a particularly rich passage from a story (any story) and have students locate and circle all adjectives. You may want to do a passage with them as guided practice and then give them another passage to do as independent practice. After allowing students to work on it as seatwork, go back and review it so they receive same-day feedback. Students benefit from doing this kind of practice daily for several days. You will not want to begin to record a grade until the student is demonstrating good understanding in daily practice.

As students do their own writing, you can encourage them to: "Make me see what you saw." "Make me feel what you feel."

DITTO #178, PRACTICE WITH ADJECTIVES

Directions: Circle each adjective.
(<u>Guided Practice</u>)

It was a huge, old barn. When you went inside there was the wonderful sweet smell of new-mown hay. Inside one stall was Annie, a gentle cow with big, chocolate-colored eyes. Her soft moos gave me a sure sign that she liked me. In the next stall, the plow horse made crinch, crunching sounds while eating the apple Uncle Jim gave him. Six white sheep and one black sheep occupied another stall. Sun streamed in through a hole in the roof. I sat down on a gunny sack. A quiet peaceful feeling rolled over me.

_____

(<u>Independent Practice</u>: Try to find at least 12 adjectives. If you can find 15 you are really sharp!)

It was a cold, wintry evening. A small, brown shaggy puppy hid under the dark belly of an automobile trying to get out of the driving snowstorm. He could hear the slish, sloshing sound of cars as they passed in the slushy snow. His growling and hurting stomach reminded him he had not eaten in way too long. He wished he was still lying next to the warm, soft body of his mother with a full stomach. How he missed the rough, tumbling play of his ten sisters and brothers.

Recognizing Key Words/Using an Index

Textbooks in science, social studies, and health often have questions at the end of the chapters and it is customary for students to be asked to write the answers. For LD students, this task seems impossible because they cannot do it in the time limits usually given. You can, however, help them develop skills that will allow them to be successful with this kind of task.

First, the students must read the question and locate the key words. For example:

How did railroads influence the growth of industry in the United States after 1860?

Ask the students, **"What do they want to know about?"** Students answer with one or two words. With a little guided practice done orally with the whole class, most students pick up this skill rapidly. (*Clue:* The key word is almost always a noun.) "In this question, the key word is railroad."

Next, have them look in the Index of the book for the heading that might look like this:

Railroads, development of, 327, 408-409

first transcontinental railroad, 327

influence on industry, 408

At this point the students will usually pick up on the secondary word *industry* and can scan page 408 for the answer to the question, eliminating the need for them to read the entire chapter to find the answer.

You may react by saying, **"But I want my students to read the entire chapter!"** Many good students report that they do not read every word. It is not uncommon for college professors to assign outrageously long reading assignments; thus, these students have had to develop techniques whereby they can get the assignment done in the time frame allowed. If we do not teach LD students to use the same techniques, we are placing them at a disadvantage because they will not be able to compete with the good students.

Note that no special materials are included for teaching this crucial skill. It is most effectively taught by having LD students use the regular class texts/indexes in science and social studies.

Have them read one of the questions aloud, tell you the key word, and then look up that key word in the index. Next, have the students turn to the designated page in the text and scan for the key word in the text. Then the students read everything in the paragraph where the key word appears.

If the students do not find the needed information in the text, it is probably because they have used the wrong key word. Have them try another noun from the question.

Note-Taking

The skill of note-taking is essential for success in school because of its dual roles of increasing comprehension and clarifying written communication. It is suggested that LD students have at least twice weekly practice using this skill—beginning as soon as they reach a functional level of third grade (this generally happens around fifth or sixth grade) and continuing every year through high school. For LD students planning to proceed to college, it is recommended they have at least two semesters in twelfth grade of intense practice using the skills involved with note-taking.

There are two forms of note-taking that need to be taught:

a. making notes while reading/studying
b. making notes while listening to lecture

Making notes from printed material for study purposes is by far easier than taking notes while listening. When listening the material is lost almost immediately so if the student's auditory memory is poor, or the individual is a slow note-taker, it is unlikely the student will gain much from the lecture format. Happily, however, students with these problems can improve their ability to listen and to take notes.

When teaching students to take notes, begin by teaching them to take notes from written material. Using short reading passages, have students:

a. Read the passage twice.
b. Locate and write the main idea.
c. Locate and write the supporting details.

For example, *read* the following passage twice:

> There are two kinds of trees—deciduous and evergreen. Deciduous trees lose their leaves in winter while evergreens are green year round. Some examples of trees that lose their leaves are oak, elm, and fruit trees. Some examples of evergreens are pines and cedars.

Instruct the student to extract the main idea and supporting details and write them:

I. There are two kinds of trees
   A. Deciduous lose leaves   (58 letters)
   B. Evergreen do not

Later you will want to show students how to reduce the number of words they write without losing the meaning:

I. trees—2 kinds
    deciduous lose leaves   (46 letters)
    evergreens don't

Later you can teach students to develop their own form of shorthand to use in note-taking. Begin the lesson by writing on the board:

2 da we r 2 lrn to rit fstr

Say, **"As soon as you can read what this says, raise your hand."** (When the majority of hands are up, have the students read each word as you point to it.) Say, **"It is helpful to be able to make notes quickly. Can you explain how this skill might be useful to you?"**

Let students know that good students take notes and you will teach them this skill so they can get better grades. Note-taking is a very individualized matter. Each person develops his or her own system of shorthand for personal note-taking. The only requirement is that the person needs to be able to read back what he or she wrote! Many people drop the vowels when they take notes or they develop symbols that stand for words they use a lot. Here are some examples:

u hv a nis dog. wht knd is sh?	Cn we go 2 sho 2 nit?	Pepl ned 2 drnk 8 glss H_2O/da.

<u>Answers:</u> You have a nice dog. What kind is she?

Can we go to (the) show tonight?

People need to drink eight glasses (of) water each day.

When teaching students to take notes, use their regular texts. Give them paragraphs to *outline* the main idea and the supporting details and then ask them to go back and reduce the number of letters in their outline by using their own shorthand. Before they start, let them know they will need to be able to read the notes to you.

There are some interesting spinoffs from having students do these activities. First, they seem to improve in their spelling and look at words more closely. When they are trying to decide which letters they'll have to keep and which ones they can leave out, they become more aware of how words are spelled. Second, if they are taking notes on materials they will be tested on, such as social studies and science, they usually get a better score on the test. The reason for this is that as they write the notes in both formats, the extra exposure to the information is bnefishl (you know, beneficial).

To teach students to do note-taking while listening, begin by selecting short paragraphs to read to them—preferably simple paragraphs that talk about things that readily convert to mental images. For example:

It snowed last night. The ground was covered with a thick blanket of white. Four children wearing yellow coats and red mittens were skating on the frozen pond.

Note: **M.I.** 4. kids r ice skating.

At the start of the race, Mary could not keep up with Jon because he ran too fast. But as they reached the 15-mile mark, Jon was so tired he could barely jog, so Mary overtook him and won.

Note: **M.I.** Mary won a long race.

In the beginning talk a bit more slowly than usual because students need time to get their notes on paper. Go around the room and give encouragement—"Good," "That's right!" "Wow!" You may also want to reread selections during the first few days. At first, do not put grades on students' work because it may be discouraging.

As students get proficient in extracting the main idea, choose paragraphs that are a bit more complicated, such as those with a main idea and one or two supporting details. For example:

> Near San Francisco, artists have built some really unusual sculptures. Using pieces of driftwood and old stuff that was just dumped, they have made a boat, a castle and a huge hand.
>
> *Notes:* **M.I.** Artists built sculptures near S.F. from junk.

> The Civil War lasted from 1861 to 1865. The Union soldiers came from the north while the Confederate Army was made up of soldiers from the south.
>
> *Notes:* **M.I.** The Civil War lasted 4 years.
> North = Union Army
> South = Confederate Army

Students grow in their ability to exercise this skill so be patient and continue to provide regular experiences. You will get the most growth (and the quickest growth) if you do an activity daily. Choose paragraphs from their regular texts, from the encyclopedia, from the newspaper, or from Barnell-Loft's *Multiple Skills* (items requiring no additional purchases).

Paragraph Writing

Fourth grade is an ideal time to teach students how to write paragraphs. By that point they have mastered the prerequisite skills:

- They know the elements of a good sentence.
- They have adequate spelling skills.
- They understand and apply capitalization/punctuation skills.

Unfortunately, most LD students are not ready to write paragraphs in fourth grade because their skills development is only at grade 2.0-2.5. It is important, therefore, that teachers in the later elementary grades and junior high reteach basic paragraph writing.

First, students must know what a paragraph is. *A paragraph is a group of sentences that tells about one main idea or topic.* They need to be able to look at someone else's writing and determine whether it meets this standard.

Next, they need to be able to look at several sentences, organizing them into logical order and writing them in a paragraph format.

Finally, they need to be able to take a topic and write a sensible paragraph.

Dittoes #184 through 191 can be made into a student workbook designed to teach this skill. As a group, help students to read and discuss each page and to do the activities suggested.

Name _____

DITTO #179, PARAGRAPH WORKBOOK

A paragraph is a group of sentences that tells about one main idea or topic.

    Look at the paragraphs below. They were written by two students. One paragraph tells about one topic, while the other talks about more than one topic. Can you tell which one is correct?

-1- My favorite kind of animal is a dog. Dogs are friendly. You can teach dogs tricks.

-2- My favorite animal is the cat. I also like dogs and horses. My best friend has a horse. His name is Star and he loves apples.

    If you picked paragraph one, you were right. Everything in that paragraph was about dogs. Sometimes, students think the longer the paragraph is, the better it is. Someone always asks how many sentences should a paragraph have. Can you make a guess? Write your guess here. Don't let anyone else see it.

_____

    Now let's take a look at some paragraphs from your books. Turn to page _____

in your _____ book. A paragraph begins where the print is indented and continues to where the next indention occurs. Let's count together how many sentences are in each paragraph on this page.

DITTO #180, PARAGRAPH WORKBOOK

We found paragraphs ranging from _____ sentences to _____ sentences.

   A paragraph is always indented. Indent means to move the first line over from the margin of the paper.
   Here are some sentences. Can you number them in proper order?

_____ She got out all the ingredients.

_____ Dad asked mother to bake some homemade bread.

_____ Mom went to the kitchen.

_____ She mixed flour, water, and yeast and let the dough rise.

_____ Dad said that the bread was the best he had ever tasted.

_____ She put the dough in the oven to bake.

   Now write the sentences in paragraph format on the lines below. You will note the first line is indented.

_____

_____

_____

_____

_____

_____

_____

Name _____

DITTO #181, PARAGRAPH WORKBOOK

   Sentences in a paragraph must be in the correct order. The first sentence usually tells the main idea of the paragraph and the other sentences give supporting details.
   Read the paragraph below.

> Puerto Rico is a beautiful island. It is about 1,000 miles southeast of Florida. It has a nice climate, sandy beaches, and wonderful hotels. These things make Puerto Rico a great place to visit.

   The first sentence tells you that the paragraph is about the island of Puerto Rico. This is the main idea. The other sentences tell you more about the island.
   In the next paragraph, the sentences are not in the correct order. Can you figure out how they should go? Write the paragraph as it should be. Don't forget to indent!

> He claimed the island for Spain. Spain then gave the island to the United States in 1898. Christopher Columbus is believed to have landed on the island in 1493.

_____

_____

_____

© 1995 by The Center for Applied Research in Education

Name _____

DITTO #182, PARAGRAPH WORKBOOK

<u>All sentences in a paragraph should relate to the main idea.</u> (Remember that the main idea usually comes either first or last in the paragraph.) Even good authors sometimes forget that all sentences in a paragraph should go with the main idea. In each paragraph on this page, one sentence does not fit. Can you find it? Cross out the sentence that does not belong.

When we think of pumpkins we usually think of Halloween and jack-o'-lanterns. Did you know that the pulp (inside) of the pumpkin is a vegetable that is very good for us? To make it taste good, we boil it with a little water, sugar, cinnamon, and nutmeg. Spinach is also a vegetable.

Have you ever dreamed of being rich? Maybe someday you will be. Read some books about buried treasure. Read other books as well. If you live in California, maybe you will find a gold mine. If you live in Florida, maybe you will find a pirate's plunder. Some Civil War soldiers buried $350,000 worth of stolen jewelry in Virginia.

Lions live in groups called "prides." The group is like a big family. There are usually two or three grown male lions and several females with their cubs. The mother lion carries her baby by the nape of the neck. The lions show affection for each other by rubbing against each other.

About a hundred years ago, some children were playing in the sandy bed of a dried-up river. One boy found a stick. One found a rock. Since it was somewhat different from other rocks he had seen, he took it home. It turned out to be a "blue stone" diamond. Immediately, Africans began exploiting their land. Africa produces most of the world's diamonds.

DITTO #183, PARAGRAPH WORKBOOK

Let's review what we have learned so far.

- A paragraph is a group of sentences about one topic or idea.

- The main idea usually comes first.

- Other sentences in the paragraph tell more about the main idea.

- The sentences in a paragraph must fall in an order so they make sense.

Directions: Using the sentences below, arrange them in correct order by putting the main idea first. Indent.

_____ On one, I put peanut butter.

_____ I decided to make a sandwich.

_____ On the other, I put jelly.

_____ I got out two slices of bread.

_____ When I got home from school, I was really hungry.

_____ I watched T.V. while I ate.

_____

_____

_____

_____

_____

_____

Normally you write paragraphs on lined notebook paper. Your teacher will show you (on the overhead) how to place the words from the paragraph above on regular notebook paper. Your teacher will also explain about margins.

Name _____

DITTO #184, PARAGRAPH WORKBOOK

Here are other sentences for organizing in correct order and writing paragraphs on notebook paper:

_____ The lake froze over.

_____ Tony decided to walk on the ice.

_____ He yelled for help and neighbors were able to help him.

_____ It was very cold last night.

_____ Suddenly, the ice gave way.

_____ Tony fell into the deep water.

- -

_____ She said we could trim it.

_____ First, we put on the lights.

_____ Mother bought a Christmas tree.

_____ Finally, we added the tinsel.

_____ Next, we added the colored balls.

_____ It looked wonderful when we were all finished.

- -

_____ I went back to sleep.

_____ The clock went off.

_____ Mother called me several times.

_____ I was too tired to get up.

_____ Still, I couldn't get up.

_____ A cold, wet wash rag hit my face and—suddenly—I was wide awake.

DITTO #185, PARAGRAPH WORKBOOK

Look at the picture. It shows many different things happening.

    Write a paragraph of at least four sentences that tells about the picture. You can use this topic sentence to help you get started.

Mrs. Smiths store is on fire. _____

_____

_____

_____

_____

_____

_____

_____

_____

Name _____

DITTO #186, PARAGRAPH WORKBOOK

Directions: Using the topic sentence given, write a paragraph by adding at least three supporting details.

Taking good care of your teeth is important. _____

_____

_____

_____

_____

_____

Some dogs can be taught to do tricks. _____

_____

_____

_____

_____

_____

My favorite holiday is _____

_____

_____

_____

_____

_____

Name _____

DITTO #187, PARAGRAPH WORKBOOK

Directions: Using the topic sentence given, write a paragraph by adding at least four supporting details.

The country that I would most like to visit is _____

_____

_____

_____

_____

_____

Many people have hobbies or things they like to do in their spare time. _____

_____

_____

_____

_____

_____

Can a girl and boy be best friends? _____

_____

_____

_____

_____

_____

_____

Name _____

DITTO #188, PARAGRAPH WORKBOOK

Directions: Using the main idea given below, write at least three supporting details.

If Only

Someone asked me, "What would you do if you won a million dollars?" _____

_____

_____

_____

_____

_____

_____

_____

Using a cluster can be helpful in organizing your ideas. Here is a sample cluster.

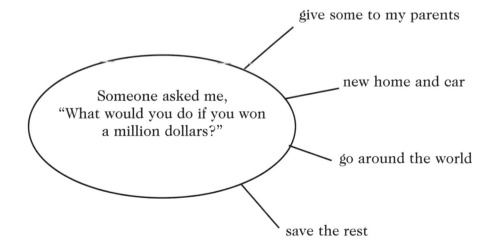

Name _____

DITTO #189, PARAGRAPH WORKBOOK

Directions: Using the main idea given below, write at least three supporting details. You may write about a dog you know or an imaginary dog. A space has been left at the beginning of the sentence to allow you to name the dog.

One Smart Dog

_____ must be the world's smartest dog because he can do so many

tricks. _____

_____

_____

_____

_____

_____

_____

_____

Cluster: <u>Name 3 tricks</u>

_____ must be the world's smartest dog because he can do so many tricks.

Name _____

DITTO #190, PARAGRAPH WORKBOOK

Directions: Using the sentence starter given below, write a paragraph that is at least four sentences long. A space has been left at the top so you may enter a title.

Have you ever been homesick? _____

_____

_____

_____

_____

_____

_____

_____

_____

_____

Cluster: _____   Describe what the circumstances
                          were or what symptoms you felt.

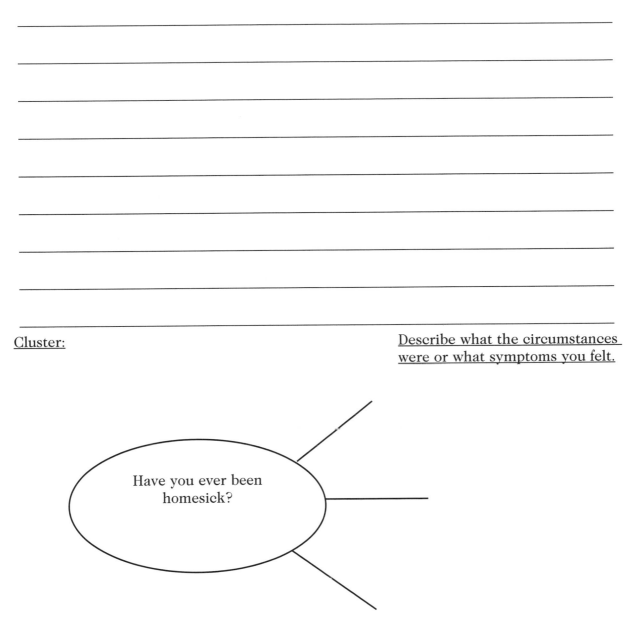

Have you ever been
homesick?

Name _____

DITTO #191, PARAGRAPH WORKBOOK,
STUDENT CHECKLIST FOR WRITING PARAGRAPHS

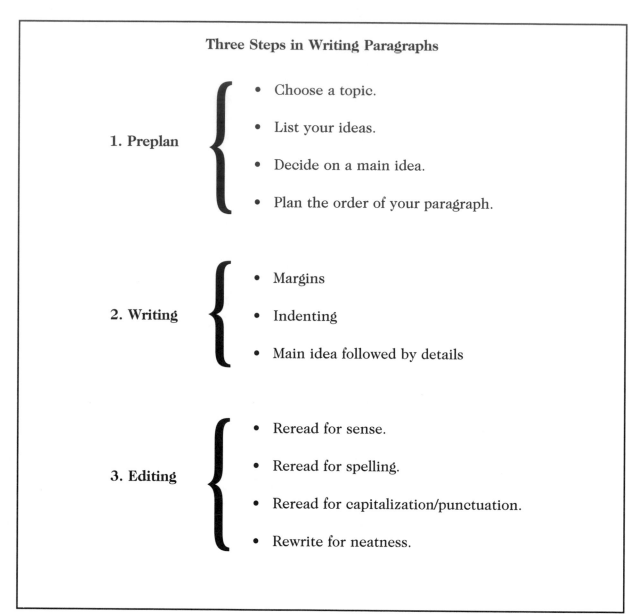

Three Steps in Writing Paragraphs

1. Preplan
- Choose a topic.
- List your ideas.
- Decide on a main idea.
- Plan the order of your paragraph.

2. Writing
- Margins
- Indenting
- Main idea followed by details

3. Editing
- Reread for sense.
- Reread for spelling.
- Reread for capitalization/punctuation.
- Rewrite for neatness.

REPORT WRITING

Having mastered note-taking and paragraph writing, students are ready to learn how to write a report. I have seen teachers tell students they must write a several-page report on ... and turn it in by .... Students have no idea how to do it so they ask for parental help. Parents may not have any idea of how to do it either or may have no time to help. The result: The student either fails to do the assignment, copies directly from a book, or turns in an assignment of poor quality. This is why it is imperative that you provide the students with guidance every step of the way as they have their initial five experiences with report writing.

In the beginning, reports should be short (about one page). During early report-writing efforts, assign the same topic to all students. You will also want to give them an outline of topics to cover. As a group, guide them through finding the information they will need for the report. Together, read aloud and make notes about the subject. You can put notes on the acetates of the overhead projector while students can put them on index cards—one card for each major topic on the outline. On the top of each index card, students put the number of the topic to which the notes apply.

Dittoes #192 through 196 offer outlines for five guided practice reports: Hummingbirds, The Heart, Healthy Living Practices, State or Country, and Electricity. Your school library should have adequate information on these topics.

Hummingbirds

I. Characteristics of Hummingbirds
   A. Size
   B. Color
   C. Beak
   D. Flight patterns

II. Habitat
   A. Where do they live?
   B. What do they eat?

III. Reproduction
   A. Describe their nests
   B. How many eggs?
   C. How long before babies can survive on their own?

**DITTO #193, STUDENT NOTEBOOK HANDOUT,
REPORT-WRITING PRACTICE**

The Heart

I.   Characteristics of the heart

A. Muscle

B. Pumps oxygenated blood through body

C. Size/weight

D. Location

II. How does the blood circulate?

A. Right auricle

B. Right ventricle

C. Lungs

1. release of Co_2

2. oxygenation of blood

D. Left auricle

E. Left ventricle

F. Arteries

G. Capillaries

H. Veins

Healthy Living Practices

I.   Why do we need to take care of our body?
    A. Live longer
    B. Feel better
    C. Greater energy
II. What should we eat?
    A. Number of calories needed
    B. Best foods to eat
    C. What foods to avoid
    D. The importance of water
        1. How much water should we drink?
III. How much sleep is needed?
IV. The importance of exercise
    A. What kind of exercise?
    B. How much exercise?

State or Country

I. Describe the state or country

A. Size

    1. area

    2. population

B. Location

C. Types of terrain

D. Climate

E. Importance

II. Economy

A. Natural resources

B. Products produced

    1. agricultural

    2. manufacturing

III. Interesting places to see

Name _____

Electricity

I. What is it?

   A. Flow of electrons

   B. Can do work for us

   C. Examples of its usefulnesss

II. How is electricity made?

   A. Copper wire, magnets

III. Where is electricity made?

   A. Waterways and dams

   B. Steam generated

   C. Nuclear energy plants

IV. Safety rules to make it safer

   A. Protecting small children from outlets

   B. Replacing frayed cords

   C. Avoiding contact between water and electricity

   D. Circuit breakers

   E. Insulators

When you have guided the students through their research on one of the subjects and they are ready to write, they need to see each Roman numeral represents a different paragraph:

Hummingbirds—3 paragraphs

The Heart—2 paragraphs

Healthy Living Practices—4 paragraphs

State or Country—3 paragraphs

Electricity—4 paragraphs

Place the students in pairs. Have them write the first paragraph, then ask their partner to read it before turning it in. It is the partner's job to tell the student if it doesn't make sense or if he or she sees obvious errors. When you correct it, remember that egos are fragile in the beginning, so you want to give encouragement to keep students writing. If the paragraph is glaringly or horribly inferior, rewrite it on a different piece of paper as it should be and have the student orally read to you what you wrote. Ask whether the student wants to keep his or her original paragraph for the portfolio or use yours (in which case, you keep both).

The next day, the students can do the second paragraph. When all paragraphs are complete, combine them into a single report. Have the pairs read the entire report before handing it in, cautioning them to watch for redundancies. (LD students are much more likely to be willing to write reports if they are allowed to use word processors; this way, correction does not require the students to rewrite the paper.)

You can use the five outlines given here to make other similar reports. For example, if you want to have students write about an animal, help them adapt the <u>Hummingbirds</u> outline pattern so it fits the snake, the cougar, etc. <u>The Heart</u> outline pattern can be altered to fit a report on <u>The Digestive System</u> or <u>The Nervous System</u>. The <u>State or Country</u> outline can be reused multiple times at all upper age levels. Using the adaptations of these three outlines, you can have students continue their report-writing practice. The quality of the students' performance will gradually improve over time if experiences are frequently provided. Give students a copy of the outlines to keep in their notebook. In later years they may want to refer back to them.

When students have gotten fairly proficient at writing a report from an outline you provide, the next step is to get them to do the entire process from scratch—research a topic, take notes, develop an outline, and write the report independently.

To teach students to develop an outline, you may want to have them take a piece of writing and try to see if they can figure out the author's outline—main idea and supporting details. You can use a page from a text or you can use the Upper-Grade Reading Passages given at the beginning of this unit.

On Dittoes #197 through 201, you will find bulletin board materials to go with this section on report writing. These dittoes give the steps a person needs to go through in writing reports from scratch on a variety of subjects. *Science*, for example, offers multiple opportunities for report writing. When studying about light there are many smaller topics that can be assigned for report writing, such as "Refraction of Light Rays" or "How Does the Eye Work?" When studying sound students might be asked to write a report on what causes echoes. Likewise, *history* offers many subtopics to write about. When the unit on the first settlers in America occurs, you might want to have students do a report on the Quaker Religion. When the Revolutionary War is studied, students might write reports on such subtopics as the Boston Tea Party or the Declaration of Independence.

Show students how to complete a report with a colorful cover, title page, pictures, or charts. Neat papers *do* get better grades, so the first impression the teacher gets very much influences the final grade assigned.

LD students find report writing very difficult because it requires them to use so many skills—note-taking, organization, spelling, mechanics. You will want to acknowledge that you know this is hard for them and to show your appreciation for their willingness to keep trying. Let them know you had trouble with this skill when you were young and that they will get better at it as they get older. Practice *does* make perfect.

PREWRITING

Choose a topic.
List your ideas.
Make a plan:
    number the ideas in the order they should come

WRITE A FIRST DRAFT

Use every other line.

REVISE

Read your work.
Make needed changes.
Ask your partner to read your paper and to make
suggestions.

PUBLISH AND SHARE

COPY your work neatly.
Proofread and correct.
SHARE what you learned.

PROOFREADING CHECKLIST

Read for sense.
Check all spelling.
Check for capitals and periods.
Check for appearance.

Name _____

DITTO #202, WRITING STORIES (REVISITED)

Directions: Write a short story. Include a beginning, middle, and end.

The First Time I Drove

_____

_____

_____

_____

_____

_____

_____

_____

_____

_____

Name _____

DITTO #203, WRITING STORIES (REVISITED)

Directions: Write a short story. Include a beginning, middle, and end.

Bill and Sue

_____

_____

_____

_____

_____

_____

_____

_____

Name _____

DITTO #204, WRITING STORIES (REVISITED)

Directions: Write a short story. Include a beginning, middle, and end.

The Trials of Babysitting

_____

_____

_____

_____

_____

_____

_____

_____

_____

UNDERSTANDING ANALOGIES

In education we want to teach children to think critically, and analogies offer an opportunity to do that. As you look at a pair of words, you seek the relationship between the two words. Then you must find a similar relationship between two other words. Dittoes #205 through 210 offer activity sheets that ask students to seek these relationships. Several kinds of relationships can exist:

- the words can be synonyms
- the words can be antonyms
- action-to-object relationship
- object-to-place relationship
- numerical relationship
- relationship of traits

When you begin using these sheets, do the first two as a guided practice activity, teaching the students to read them correctly and stopping to discuss why particular answers are correct.

After you have gone through several of the activity sheets as a group, you may want to pair the students to do the others or use them as seatwork with a follow-up discussion. If you are sure the students understand the concepts and will not need parental help, the sheets could also be given as homework.

Ditto #205

1. six
2. out
3. night
4. read
5. cool
6. work
7. bark
8. puppy
9. grass
10. no

Ditto #206

1. foot
2. fall
3. dime
4. green
5. yard

6. finish
7. eat
8. sister
9. deaf
10. sewing

Ditto #207

1. adult
2. kitchen
3. dollar
4. bottom
5. sad, mad, unhappy
6. yellow
7. fast
8. food
9. large
10. thermometer

Ditto #208

1. hand
2. year
3. pie
4. hard
5. finger
6. pig
7. Halloween
8. tornado, hurricane
9. female
10. small, tiny

Ditto #209

1. down
2. defeat
3. forest, woods
4. rough
5. princess

6. shape
7. arm
8. day
9. noon
10. boat

Ditto #210

1. last
2. December
3. cut
4. father
5. food
6. difficult
7. jar
8. cool
9. sweet
10. page, unit, chapter

Name _____

DITTO #205, ANALOGIES ACTIVITY SHEET

Example 1—Here is a set of words:

   chair : sit   ::   bed : _____. We read it as:

"Chair is to sit   as   bed is to lie."

The relationship here is what we call object-to-purpose. We use chairs for sitting and beds when we want to lie down.

Example 2—Here is another set of words:

   ship : water   ::   train : _____. We read it as:

"Ship is to water   as   train is to track."

The relationship is object-to-place. A ship goes on the water while a train runs on a track.

Directions: Here are ten sets. Try to supply the missing words. Your teacher will go over the answers with you. Treat it like a game. Give yourself 10 points for each correct answer. See if you can improve your score each time you play.

1. two   :   four   ::   three   : _____.

2. open   :   close   ::   in   : _____.

3. light   :   day   ::   dark   : _____.

4. paper   :   write   ::   book   : _____.

5. hot   :   cold   ::   warm   : _____.

6. come   :   go   ::   play   : _____.

7. duck   :   quack   ::   dog   : _____.

8. cat   :   dog   ::   kitten   : _____.

9. white   :   snow   ::   green   : _____.

10. ten   :   net   ::   on   : _____.

Did you learn anything new? If so, GOOD for YOU!

Name _____

DITTO #206, ANALOGIES ACTIVITY SHEET

Example 1—Here is a set of words:

time : watch :: inch : _____. We read it as:

"Time is to watch as inch is to ruler."

The relationship is purpose-to-object. We use a watch to tell the time while we use a ruler to measure inches.

Example 2—Here is another set of words:

Food : you :: gas : _____. We read it as:

"Food is to you as gas is to vehicle."

The relationship is object-to-object. You need food to run just as a vehicle must have gas to run.

Directions: Here are ten sets. Try to supply the missing words. Your teacher will go over the answers with you. Have fun. Make it a game. Give yourself 10 points for each correct answer.

1. mitten : hand :: boot : _____.

2. summer : winter :: spring : _____.

3. five : ten :: nickel : _____.

4. stop : go :: red : _____.

5. school : playground :: house : _____.

6. begin : end :: start : _____.

7. water : drink :: food : _____.

8. boy : brother :: girl : _____.

9. see : hear :: blind : _____.

10. pan : cooking :: needle : _____.

© 1995 by The Center for Applied Research in Education

DITTO #207, ANALOGIES ACTIVITY SHEET

Example 1—Here is a set of words:

    clothes : closet ::   books : _____. We read it as:

"Clothes are to closet as   books are to shelf."

The relationship here is object-to-place. We use a closet as a place for clothes and we keep our books on a shelf, in a bookcase, or locker.

Example 2—Here is another set of words:

    low : valley   ::   high   : _____. We read it as:

"Low is to valley   as   high is to mountain or hill."

The relationship has to do with traits. For a place to be labeled as a valley, it must be low; likewise, places that are high are called hills or mountains depending on how high they are.

Directions: Here are ten sets. Try to supply the missing words. Be happy!

1. young : old :: baby : _____.

2. bed : bedroom :: stove : _____.

3. one : four :: quarter : _____.

4. up : down :: top : _____.

5. smile : happy :: frown : _____.

6. sugar : white :: butter : _____.

7. drip : slow :: pour : _____.

8. shovel : dirt :: spoon : _____.

9. cup : small :: bucket : _____.

10. time : clock :: temperature : _____.

Are you getting better at this? Words are power!

DITTO #208, ANALOGIES ACTIVITY SHEET

Example 1—Here is a set of words:

    right : wrong   ::   good   : _____. We read it as:

"Right is to wrong   as   good is to bad or evil."

The relationship reflects a knowledge of both synonyms and antonyms.

Examples 2—Here is another set of words:

square : four   ::   triangle   : _____. We read it as:

"Square is to four (sides)   as   triangle is to three (sides)."

Directions: Here are ten sets. Try to supply the missing words. Your teacher will go over the answers with you. Give yourself 10 points for each correct answer.

1. toe   :   foot   ::   finger   : _____.

2. day   :   week   ::   month   : _____.

3. piece   :   cake   ::   slice   : _____.

4. cotton   :   soft   ::   rock   : _____.

5. necklace   :   neck   ::   ring   : _____.

6. hamburger   :   cow   ::   bacon   : _____.

7. heart   :   Valentines   ::   pumpkin   : _____.

8. rain   :   storm   ::   wind   : _____.

9. Popeye   :   Olive Oyl   ::   male   : _____.

10. big   :   little   ::   huge   : _____.

Did you get six or more right? If so, you are doing fine.

Name _____

DITTO #209, ANALOGIES ACTIVITIES SHEET

Example 1—Here is a set of words:

   one : two   ::   three : _____. We read it as:

"One is to two   as   three is to four/or as three is to six."

The relationship is a numerical one, either as straight counting—one, two, three, four—or two is twice as much as one, so six would be twice as much as three.

Example 2—Here is another set of words:

he : she   ::   his   : _____. We read it as:

"He is to she   as   his is to hers."

The relationship reflects antonyms.

Directions: Here are ten sets. Try your skill at finding the missing words. Your teacher will go over the answers with you. You get 10 points for each correct answer. A score of 6 makes you a master!

1. ceiling   :   floor   ::   up   :   _____.

2. win   :   lose   ::   conquer   :   _____.

3. book   :   library   ::   tree   :   _____.

4. velvet   :   smooth   ::   sandpaper :   _____.

5. king   :   queen   ::   prince   :   _____.

6. red   :   color   ::   square   :   _____.

7. foot   :   ankle   ::   hand   :   _____.

8. minute   :   hour   ::   hour   :   _____.

9. breakfast   :   morning   ::   lunch   :   _____.

10. pilot   :   plane   ::   captain   :   _____.

Name _____

DITTO #210, ANALOGIES ACTIVITY SHEET

Example 1—Here is a set of words:

    day : hour   ::   minute: _____. We read it as:

"Day is to hour   as   minute is to second."

The relationship is both temporal and whole to part. Days are made up of hours while minutes are composed of seconds.

Example 2—Here is another set of words:

    fish : pond   ::   whale : _____. We read it as:

"Fish is to pond   as   whale is to ocean/sea."

The relationship is object-to-place. Fish live in the pond but whales are only found in oceans or seas.

Directions: Here are ten sets. Can you supply correct answers for at least 8 of these? Your teacher will go over the answers with you. I hope you have enjoyed playing these word games.

1. begin   :   end   ::   first   : _____.

2. January   :   February   ::   November   : _____.

3. pencil   :   write   ::   knife   : _____.

4. girl   :   mother   ::   boy   : _____.

5. thirst   :   water   ::   hunger   : _____.

6. easy   :   simple   ::   hard   : _____.

7. milk   :   carton   ::   mayonnaise : _____.

8. heater   :   warmth   ::   fan   : _____.

9. lemon   :   sour   ::   sugar   : _____.

10. whole   :   fraction   ::   book   : _____.

6 MATERIALS FOR TEACHING ADVANCED WRITING

Writing is the area of greatest difficulty for LD students. At the lower grades students lack the knowledge of spelling and mechanics required to do sophisticated writing, but senior high school teachers will want to encourage writing because the students are so much more able to do it. Students need experience with a variety of types of writing, including:

- *Casual Writing*: This type of writing includes journal writing, friendly letters, invitations, thank-you notes, and other informal notes.
- *Business Writing*: This type of writing includes keeping a journal, résumés, business letters and letters of complaint, and how to write directions.
- *Creative Writing*: This type of writing includes writing poetry, plays and stories. Students should learn how to handle dialogue and to develop extensive vocabularies.
- *Expository Writing*: This is the type of writing most often done in school. Students should learn how to choose a topic, gather information, take notes, organize information into a meaningful whole, and put their ideas on paper in a logical way. For students planning to go on to college, you will want to provide instruction in writing term papers.
- *Persuasive Writing/Speaking*: This type of discourse involves thinking in a logical way and then coaxing others—by using well-chosen words—to see a subject from the same point of view as that of the author/speaker.

CASUAL WRITING

Casual writing usually comprises the largest part of our writing.

The Journal

Teachers frequently institute the practice of keeping a daily journal. They use it as an opening activity, providing them time to take care of early morning chores such as taking roll and collecting homework. I see two disturbing trends in the use of journals:

1. In general, student entries are not very meaningful. They tend to be short and involve little or no thinking.
2. The second shortcoming that occurs with diaries or journals is that no one reads them.

There are ways to overcome these shortcomings. To solve #1, you can give students topics or a choice of topics to write about. For example, you might give the student a scenario to react to, such as:

You are standing in line at the movie. You look down and see a five-dollar bill. Will you turn it in to the lost and found? Keep it? Explain why you made the choice you did.

The next day, try:

You see a bag on the sidewalk. You pick it up. It contains $4,000 and a bank deposit slip. Will you take it to the bank or the police? Keep it?

The answers in these cases may be very different. In the scenario involving the large amount of money, it is illegal to keep it.

Having students write in their journals at the end of the day or the end of a lesson can be very productive for both you and them. You can ask them to tell you what they learned during the lesson. For example, "Today, we talked about the digestive system in science. Tell me as much as you can about that system in 15 minutes." This kind of journal writing allows you to check for understanding/listening and gives students greater motivation to listen to lectures.

To solve #2, make arrangements for someone to read the students' entries. The students can share their entries daily with a partner whose job is to:

a. correct spelling
b. let student know if entry doesn't make sense

You might team with a teacher in another class and ask students in that class to read and respond to the journals. You could also use student monitors to read the diaries—those students who are more able and finish their work quicker than others.

You, too, can read the students' journals, if not daily, on at least a periodic schedule.

Journal writing becomes more exciting when you ask students to share particularly noteworthy selections with the class. It is not a good idea to *require* students to share; they need to be willing and what they share must be worthwhile.

After a student shares, you may want to use that sharing as a journal writing topic. "Respond to what Jenny read to you today."

Friendly Letters

Students need opportunities to write letters to friends. This is an area sadly neglected today. When friends leave, the friendships are often lost because people have forgotten or never learned the art of letter writing. Teachers can assist by using natural events to teach this skill. If a student moves away, encourage the class members to write to the student. If a teacher retires, encourage students to keep in touch. If a pupil is out ill, use the situation for letter-writing instruction. Some teachers also arrange for members of their class to exchange letters with a class at another nearby (or perhaps even distant) school.

Invitations

By the time children leave elementary school, they should be able to design a simple invitation. By the time they leave high school, they should know what information must be included.

Make up scenarios for which students design an invitation:

Birthday party	Bridal shower	Baby shower
Surprise party	Wedding	Retirement party
Anniversary party		

Figure 6–1 gives a sample instruction card you could prepare for the students.

FIGURE 6–1

Homework due Monday

Your assignment is to obtain or design an invitation for a _____.
You can bring in an invitation you have received, get a commercially-made invitation and fill it out, or make your own design. It is all right to get help from your parents. Be sure your invitation answers these questions:

<u>Who</u> is being honored?

<u>What</u> kind of celebration is it?

<u>Where</u> is the celebration occurring?

<u>When</u> (date and time) is the party?

Add any other pertinent information. For example, if you want the guests to dress casually, say so. If you do not want them to bring gifts, say, "No gifts expected." If the person being invited can bring a friend, say, "Feel free to bring a friend."

Thank-you Notes

Likewise, we need to teach students to write thank-you notes. Discuss several possible scenarios with your students, such as: writing thank-you notes for a gift received at each type of party—birthday, wedding, baby shower, retirement, etc. Students will need help in learning what to say beyond "Thanks" for the gift. They need to say why they like the gift or why the party was special.

Other Kinds of Notes

One activity that students enjoy is experiencing what it is like to be a telephone receptionist for a business. Bring in two telephones and scripts for them to enact. Get telephone note pads from your school office for students to practice the skill of taking a message. Here are two sample scripts:

Script #1

RRIIng!

RECEPTIONIST: "Hello. This is World-Wide Insurance. How may I direct your call?"

CUSTOMER: "This is Roger Merritt. My policy number is XXP261. I had a car accident today and I need to speak with a claims adjuster."

RECEPTIONIST: "All of our adjusters are busy with other customers right now. May I take your number and have an adjuster call you shortly?"

CUSTOMER: "Yes. My number is area code 213-592-8732."

RECEPTIONIST: "I will give this note to an adjuster immediately, Mr. Merritt. Your number is area code 213-592-8732?"

CUSTOMER: "That's right."

Each student in the class can write the message on a pad: At your earliest convenience, please call Roger Merritt, Policy #XXP261 re: Car accident on (date) 213-592-8732.

Script #2

RRIIng!

YOU: "Hello."

CALLER: "This is Martha Cohen. May I speak with your mother?"

YOU: "I'm sorry, Mrs. Cohen. My mother is in the shower. May I take a message and have her return your call when she gets out?"

CALLER: "I'm supposed to pick her up at 7:15 but I'm running late. I can get there by 7:45 but that will make us late to the meeting. She may want to drive her own car so she can get to the meeting on time. Please ask her to let me know what she wants to do."

YOU: "I'll have her call you as soon as she gets out of the shower. What is your number?"

CALLER   "212-663-8742."

Each student writes a note for mom.

You can also develop scripts for other scenarios:

1. Calling the school to let the teacher know why a child is absent
2. Calling to let your boss know you are going to miss work due to a death in your family and when you will be back
3. Calling 911 to report an accident with injuries (describe why you think an ambulance needs to respond)
4. Calling a friend and leaving a message with his mom regarding a job he may want to apply for (give details, where, who to see)

BUSINESS WRITING

As students become seniors, they must learn skills they will need on the job.

Some jobs require journal keeping for legal purposes. In these cases, it is extremely important for the person recording the data to be exact in the recordings because he or she may be required to testify in court at a later time, using the journal as a reminder of conversations. In these kinds of situations, you need to record dates, specific times, and word for word what was said or done.

Here is a sample script that illustrates what kind of information might be kept in such a journal:

LAWYER: "Mr. Hamaguchi, did you draw blood from the defendant on some occasion?"

WITNESS: "Yes, I did."

LAWYER: "Can you tell me where this was done?"

WITNESS: "At the County Jail."

LAWYER: "Do you remember the date you did this?"

WITNESS: "I need to consult my journal. (Looks) I drew that blood on July 5, 1994 at 5:10 P.M."

LAWYER: "How many vials did you draw?"

WITNESS: (Looks at notes) "Two."

LAWYER: "What did you do with those two vials?"

WITNESS: "I wrote the defendant's name on each vial. (Consults notes) I marked one vial with the number 6317 and the other with the number 6318. The vial marked 6317 was sent to Cellmark Labs for testing and the vial marked 6318 was sent to the Department of Justice Laboratory for testing."

With students watching, construct on the board what the entries in that journal might look like:

Defendant	Date/Time	Explanation

Writing Résumés

When you go to get a job, you may have a better chance of getting that job if you take a résumé to the interview. Résumés summarize your experience that is relevant to the position you are seeking. There are places you can go and pay to have a résumé made or you can prepare your own. Figure 6-2 shows a typical résumé pattern.

FIGURE 6–2

Résumé for
Education
Work Experience
Honors
Other Skills or Information

Sherman is applying for a job working in an automobile service department. Figure 6-3 shows how he completed his résumé.

FIGURE 6–3

Résumé for	Sherman Holmes 12077 5th Street Clanton, Arizona ph# 713-9534
Education	Graduated from Clanton High School, June 1993 Attended Valley Junior College, 1994-1995 (received a certificate as automotive repair technician)
Work Experience	Pizza House (delivery), summers 1992-1993 Service station attendant, summer 1994 (did oil change, lubes, repaired tires)
Honors	Certificate for perfect attendance, 1993
Other Skills or Information	I can make professional quality signs. I have never been arrested.

Have students fill out their own résumés. You can get them thinking about what kinds of things they could do in school *right now* that would look good on their résumé—things such as entering a work/school program or getting a job helping on a volunteer basis (at school or elsewhere).

Business Letters

While we are now able to take care of most complaints and needs by phone (thank goodness for 800 numbers), there will always be occasions when we will have to write a business letter. The sample letter shown in Figure 6–4 was written so that I could have legal proof that I had tried to resolve a problem with a company because I anticipated the possibility of having to defend my actions in court. By writing a letter and keeping a copy of it, I was able to avoid paying the amount demanded and no court action occurred. I sent the letter by U.S. certified mail so that I would receive proof that it was delivered and received.

FIGURE 6–4

124 Seventh Avenue
Eaton Falls, Kansas 02213
July 12, 1995

Oscar's Landscaping
278 Main Street
Eaton Falls, Kansas 02213

Enclosed you will find my check #457 in the amount of $375 to cover the cost of the landscaping work you did in May at my home. When you and I spoke, you gave me a verbal price of $350 and that was what I agreed to pay. I do not intend to pay the $515 stated on your bill. I called the Contractor's Board and found out you are required to give a written estimate for any work that will exceed $350. You did not give me that written estimate. My friend who was present when you said $350 is willing to testify to that effect.

Sincerely,

Figure 6–5 shows the format of a business letter.

FIGURE 6–5

Your Address
City, State ZIP Code
Date

Name of Company
Address
City, State ZIP code

message:
give particulars
state complaint
state outcome desired

salutation

Have students write letters for the following scenarios:

1. You ordered a wallet with your initials on it from the catalog put out by Oklahoma Mail Order Company, 1133 Sixth Avenue, Broken Bow, Oklahoma 75608. The wallet came with the wrong initials.
2. You are planning a trip to Utah. You write the Utah Tourist Bureau, 759 Nowhere Street, Provo, Utah 11223, requesting "any materials they think would be handy" in planning your trip.
3. You belong to The Health Fitness Gym (some address, your town) but you don't go any more. The gym will continue to bill your credit card every month for dues until you send a letter of resignation. Write that letter.

You and your students may want to think of additional scenarios. Encourage students to talk with their parents for ideas, too. You might help students construct such letters for their parents to send.

Writing or Giving Directions

This is another important life skill, for which students need multiple experiences. Begin your unit on this subject with a discussion of how good directions help us. Let students give examples of incidences where poor directions created a problem for them. You can follow with this write up:

Have you ever had trouble opening a jar? There are some tricks that can help you. (1) Try giving the lid of the jar a few sharp raps against a hard surface. (2) If that doesn't work, run very hot water over the lid (do not let the water get on the glass part of the jar). (3) If neither of these work, cover the lid with a damp dish towel and turn the lid.

Give students opportunities to write directions. Here are some scenarios you can suggest for which they write directions:

1. steps for planning and giving a birthday party
2. demonstrate and describe how to make a paper airplane
3. directions for baking cookies
4. directions for driving from one point to another (you can do this with local maps and later have the students do it again with state or national road maps)

CREATIVE WRITING

Although creative writing is difficult for LD students, carefully chosen projects can provide them with opportunities to learn and to be successful.

Poetry

To encourage students in this area, use a Japanese form called Haiku, which is easy for LD students to grasp. It also reviews their knowledge of adjectives and helps them extend their vocabularies.

Here is an example of Haiku:

> Uri, my good dog;
> Fearless, faithful and trustworthy;
> You are my best friend.

The normal format seen in Haiku is three lines. The first line always has five syllables. The second line usually contains adjectives and always contains seven syllables. The third line contains five syllables. (This 5-7-5 pattern is something most students can understand.)

In the beginning, students may give you Haiku efforts that do not contain adjectives. The following is one such example:

> I watched the seagull
> Soaring higher and higher
> Into the gray sky.

On his next effort, Jesse wrote:

> Gray and white seagull
> Circling, spiraling upward
> In the ocean mist.

(The way Jesse said circling, it had two syllables.) Encourage the students and accept their efforts.

Plays

This is an experience that LD students enjoy and can be very good for building their self-esteem.

Working in a group, show them how to convert a familiar story into a play. Have students rewrite the story in script format, learning in the process to use a separate paragraph each time a new character speaks. The next step is to let them take parts and produce the play—complete with scenery and costumes, if they wish. In one class, two plays were written for *Cinderella* and *Hansel and Gretel*. The *Cinderella* group chose not to do scenery and costumes, but rather to let the narrator tell what the set would look like:

> NARRATOR: "Cinderella *(petite, smiling girl steps forward, courtsies and steps back into line)* lives with her evil stepmother *(the character comes forward, courtsies, makes an ugly face and then steps back)*, and her two older stepsisters." *(two taller girls step up—one giggles, the other is shy)* in a cottage near the castle where a handsome prince lives *(a tall good-looking boy steps forward and bows)*.

When Cinderella was sweeping, she had no props. She simply mimicked the motion. When the mice were present, she jumped up on a stool, said, "Mice!" and—while pointing at a spot on the floor—counted "one... two..., etc."

Both groups gave many performances and got progressively better with each performance, gaining considerable confidence and lapping up the compliments of their audiences (elementary schools and nursing homes). It was a turning point for one boy who had had little interest in school. At first, he didn't want to take a part but he became the father in *Hansel and Gretel* and soon was getting lots of applause. He decided he would participate in some of the productions of the local Civic Light Opera. In that endeavor he met a man who later employed the student in his store.

Story Writing

Dittoes #211 and #212 are examples of stories. By using them as patterns, students can write similar stories based on their own experiences.

Teacher Directions for Ditto #211   There are many things you can do with this story. Here are some possibilities:

1. Use the selection for reading practice. The functional level of the selection is 4.0 to 5.0.

2. Use the selection to stimulate vocabulary development. Using the context, have the students guess the meanings of the underlined words. Allow students to use a thesaurus/dictionary to locate an appropriate synonym. Have students rewrite the sentences substituting the synonym for the underlined word. Show students these examples:

   a. As I climbed eagerly upward, I lost my footing and started to <u>drop</u> toward the ground.

   b. As luck would have it, though, my fall was broken by a large limb and I came to rest <u>straddling</u> that limb with its rough bark.

3. Have students write the main idea of each paragraph.

4. Choose a particular part of speech (perhaps pronouns) and ask students to locate and circle all the words that are pronouns and to state the referent. For example:

   Line 4—<u>they</u> means the older boys

   Line 5—<u>you</u> means anyone who was in the tree house could look out and see the whole town

   Line 6—<u>it</u> means the tree house although students can justifiably argue that it was the view that I loved

5. Ask students to write about something they did as a child that they were not supposed to do and how it came out.

Teacher Directions for Ditto #212   There are many activities students can do with this story. Here are some possibilities.

1. Use the story for reading practice. The functional level of the selection is 4.5 to 5.0.

2. Use the selection to stimulate vocabulary development. Using a dictionary/thesaurus, locate appropriate synonyms for each underlined word. Have students

rewrite the sentences substituting the synonym for the underlined word. For example, show the students these examples:

a. She was a <u>shriveled</u> old woman with more wrinkles than I have ever seen before or since I met her.

b. <u>Strangely</u> enough, her hair was gray like her name.

3. As a group locate the main idea for each paragraph and then list each supporting detail in outline form. (Since the students are not familiar with outlining, you will guide them. The purpose is the make them aware that some writers do an outline before they begin to write.)

4. Use this selection to review adjectives. Adjectives modify and describe nouns. You can have them find the adjectives that the author used with these nouns:

a. She was a _____, _____ woman with more wrinkles

b. She was a _____ woman with _____ features

c. a _____ nose

d. _____ eyes

e. ruled with an _____ hand

5. Ask students to write a profile of one of their teachers, a character from a book they've read, a relative, or someone they admire. Liberally give help with this assignment and make time when they finish to share their essays by reading them aloud to the class.

DITTO #211

Story Writing

<u>Read</u> this story. Note that paragraph one gives you the data needed in order to understand the rest of the selection (beginning). The second paragraph tells what happened (the middle), and the last paragraph tells how the situation came out (the end).

Have you ever had a tree house? The summer I turned ten was wonderful. The older boys in the neighborhood built a marvelous tree house about thirty feet up in one of those glorious oak trees so often seen in the South. They allowed us younger ones to come up. From the tree house you could look out and see the whole town. I loved it. (**beginning**)

A few weeks later, I wanted my father to see the tree house. He realized that a fall would surely result in serious injury or death. He forbade me to ever go up in it again, fearing that I would fall. (**the middle**)

Being ten and fearless, I didn't believe I'd fall so I continued to sneak up to the tree house to enjoy its pleasures. One day, as I climbed eagerly upward, I lost my footing and started to <u>plummet</u> toward the ground. As luck would have it, though, my fall was broken by a large limb and I came to rest <u>astride</u> that limb with its rough bark. (Oh! I forgot to mention earlier that I was wearing shorts that day.) That bark ripped the skin off the inner <u>aspect</u> of both my thighs, leaving me skinned and bloody. It was almost a month before the last scab came off my legs and walking was sheer <u>agony</u>. That was my last trip up that tree! I was not <u>infallible</u>! I realized that I could have died. I learned something else, too. Fathers sometime do know best.

Story Writing

<u>Read</u> this story. Note that the first paragraph gives the reader the data needed in order to understand the rest of the selection (the beginning). The second paragraph explains in more detail the traits of the person being written about (the middle), and the last paragraph brings the selection to a conclusion (the end).

I will never forget my seventh-grade teacher. Her name was Mrs. Gray. She was a <u>wizened</u> old woman with more wrinkles than I have ever seen before or since I met her. <u>Oddly</u> enough, her hair was gray like her name. She was a tiny woman with birdlike features—a hooked nose that <u>resembled</u> a beak and beady eyes that darted everywhere and missed no part of the action. She ruled that classroom with an iron hand and we were all terrified of her.

She was tough but fair. You never saw her that she did not have a 12″ ruler in her hand and she didn't have any <u>qualms</u> about laying it on us. Her rules were simple:

(1) Do your best work. (2) Don't talk. (3) Let her teach.

If you <u>violated</u> one of these rules, she hit you while you were in the act and you knew you were guilty.

She expected the best work that each student was capable of giving. Most of the time she would be with Bobby. We all knew why. He needed her help constantly in order to learn and even with all that help he still didn't do so well as most of us, but she cared about him. As for the rest of us, she knew about our special interests and would give us assignments that fit with them. For example, when it came time to write reports on the days of King Henry VIII, one girl who liked clothes was told to do a report on the clothing of the times. The son of a doctor had to do his report on the medical care available at the time. She was the best teacher I ever had. I think I learned more that year than in all the others put together.

EXPOSITORY WRITING

Expository writing is the writing you do to produce an essay, theme, or term report. Since this is a skill required of those going to college, it is wise to give students some experience with this. Begin with small papers. Require the student to do research, take notes, and make an outline before writing the paper.

For the first couple of reports, it would be a good idea for the class to do them as a group project. You can supervise the reading, guide the discussion, and help them take notes and later organize their notes. Developing an outline is a complex skill and you can demonstrate how to do that. Figure 6–6 shows a sample outline. Use it to model for the students the process of gathering and organizing information for writing a 3- to 4-page report. As an independent project you might have students use the sample as a pattern for writing a report on the Korean War or the Vietnam War.

Dittoes #213 and #214 give two short reports for students to work with. These can be used as patterns for developing reports of their own of a similar nature, such as a biography or short theme.

NOTE: Do students need to be introduced to the skills of footnoting and making a bibliography? At the high school level, it is important that LD students are "aware" of these, and understand the concept of plagiarism and how to avoid it.

FIGURE 6–6

Outline for a report on World War II (1939-1945)

I. Introduction
   A. When—1939–1945
   B. Who
      1. Axis Powers—Japan, Germany, and Italy
      2. Allied Powers—Great Britain, France, United States, and Russia
   C. Outcome of the war

II. Before the War
   A. Hitler, Germany, and Nazism
   B. Mussolini, Italy, and Facism
   C. Military leaders acting in the name of the Emperor, Japan, and the Rise of Militarism
   D. Efforts to avert the war

III. Events That Led to War
   A. Japan invades Manchuria (1931) and China (1937)
   B. Italy invades Ethiopia (1935)
   C. Germany annexes Austria (1938) and invades Poland (1939)

IV. War Begins
   A. France and Great Britain declare war against Axis Powers
   B. United States' efforts to remain neutral/isolated
      1. building an army
   C. Bombing of Pearl Harbor/U.S. enters war

V. War
   A. In Europe
   B. In the Pacific

VI. End of the War
   A. Germany surrenders
   B. Truman uses the atomic bomb on Japan/Japan surrenders
   C. Terms of occupation

Teacher Directions for Ditto #213   There are many things you can do with this story. Here are some possibilities:

1. Use the selection for reading practice. The functional level of the selection is 4.0 to 5.0.

2. Use the selection to increase vocabulary. Using a thesaurus or dictionary, have students locate a suitable synonym for each underlined word. Students can be asked to rewrite the sentence containing the underlined word, substituting the synonym for the underlined word. Show the students this example: ... he is best remembered for his <u>unbelieveable</u> ability to escape from all sorts of shackles...

3. Write the main idea of each paragraph.

4. You may want to teach an initial lesson on how to use phrases in conjunction with a sentence in order to give additional information. You will want to point out examples of this technique from this selection and also the fact that those phrases are separated from the sentence through the use of the comma.

5. Ask students to use this pattern to write a short report about a famous individual. Do this until students master this kind of report, which usually takes about ten experiences.

Teacher Directions for Ditto #214   There are many things you can do with this report. Here are some possibilities:

1. Use the selection for reading practice. The functional level is 4.0 to 5.0.

2. Use the underlined words for vocabulary development.

3. Ask students to find at least five phrases and circle them. Then, as a group, using an overhead projector, have students tell you what they have circled.

4. As gruesome as it seems, you will find that students are fascinated by the bizarre. You can get them to read and write about topics that exploit the bizarre. Some of the topics that interest them include voo-doo, Frankenstein's monster, the wives of Henry VIII, and the loss of Van Gogh's ear.

Report Writing

Read this story. Note that the first paragraph explains who Harry Houdini was and what he was famous for. The second and third paragraph give additional information regarding him. You can use this pattern whenever you must write a report regarding a well-known person.

Harry Houdini (hoo Dee nee) was one of the greatest magicians of all time. While he did all kinds of magic tricks, he is best remembered for his incredible ability to escape from all sorts of shackles—straight jackets, ropes, chains and locks, handcuffs, leg irons, and boxes that had been locked or nailed shut. (**beginning**)

Born in 1874 in Europe, he joined a circus as a young boy. At first, he was a trapeze performer but later he took up magic. By the time his parents brought him to the United States, he was a good-enough magician at the age of seventeen that he could earn his living that way. With his brother as a partner, he perfected the trick of escaping from a box. He began to boast, "No restraint can hold me!" He kept trying more dangerous and difficult tricks until everyone agreed he was the world's best escape artist. (**middle**)

Harry Houdini died in 1926 when, at the age of 52, a fan punched him in the stomach. Though in great pain, he insisted on finishing the performance that night. After the show, he went to the hospital but it was too late. Physicians were not able to save his life. Today's magicians are still replicating his famous tricks. Fortunately, he left writings explaining how he did a lot of the escapes, but he took the secret of some to his grave. (**end**)

Report Writing

<u>Read</u> this report. Again, we are using the three-paragraph format. The first paragraph gives you an overview of the contents of the report (beginning). The second paragraph gives additional facts (middle), and the third paragraph winds up the report (end).

People have been fascinated for centuries with the burial practices of the ancient Egyptians. These people, who lived five thousand years ago, believed in a life after death. Because of this belief, it was important to them that the body not be allowed to decay. They invented a method for preserving the body of the deceased called "mummification."

<u>Modern</u> funeral directors and embalmers do not know how to do this. From pictures found on the walls of <u>tombs</u>, we do know some of the steps used in the process. After death, the body was washed. The internal organs, such as the heart and the brain, were removed and placed in a separate container which was placed in the tomb. The body was then <u>immersed</u> in a mixture of substances for a period of 70 days. Herein lies the mystery—what substances did they use? After the 70-day period, the corpse was wrapped in many layers of cloth and placed in a sarcophagus. Sometimes this sarcophagus was placed within a larger one. The sarcophagus containing the <u>deceased</u> was placed in the tomb.

The tomb also contained beds, chairs, jewelry, baskets of food, and <u>flagons</u> of wine because they would be needed by the person in the next life. Small statues called "ushabti" were also placed there. It was believed these statues came to life and would be the servants of the dead. These funerary practices have been discovered by archeologists.

Before abandoning the expository form of writing you may want to spend some time with *news reporting* by helping students become aware of the elements that must be covered: who? what? where? when? why? outcome? significance? Have students listen to the television news and read articles in news magazines and newspapers to analyze these for answers to these questions. You might ask students to put together a class newspaper to show their understanding.

PERSUASIVE WRITING AND SPEAKING

Students enjoy and benefit from learning to use logic and critical thinking to support their arguments and opinions. Give students the chance to work on projects that involve writing persuasive essays, participating in debates, developing and delivering a sales pitch, or drawing and wording a persuasive advertisement.

Persuasive Essays

To make students aware of this type of work, you may want to develop an essay as a class. One topic students enjoy collecting data on and writing about is: "Unidentified Flying Objects Do Exist."

Debates

The essential ingredient of debate is that what is said should be based on knowledge. The basis of debating is factual; opinions are not given. Opposing views on a controversial subject are presented by teams (two to each team). In preparing for a debate, students must collect data (read and take notes) and decide how they will present it in an organized fashion and within a time frame set by the teacher. They learn to speak and think on their feet.

Students enjoy debating, particularly if it relates to subjects that are of interest to them. Try the following topics:

Women Make Better Leaders Than Men

Murderers Should Receive the Death Penalty

Abortion Should Be Illegal

Marijuana Is a More Dangerous Drug Than Alcohol

Developing and Delivering a Sales Pitch

In this activity students try to talk you into buying a specific product. Done properly, students are again exposed to and become aware of the adjectives that are used to solicit our attention and interest in a product.

Ask students to prepare a speech (and give demonstration) to persuade you to buy a product.

You may want to extend this part of the unit by examining ads in magazines for how professional salespeople appeal to you and your senses with both pictures and words. Students may then want to develop their own picture ads for fictional or real products.